Stories

from the

Yogic Heart

Edited by Lisa Miriam Cherry

Yogic Heart Publishing
www.yogicheart.com
Box 54511 Toronto, Ont.
Canada M5M 4N5

Copyright © 2010 Lisa M. Cherry
Compilation and editing: Lisa M. Cherry
Interior Layout: Dave Henry
Beaded Heart Photo: Tom Richardson
Flower photo montage and yellow scarf photo: Charles Buchwald
Audio transcribers: Joanne Holtvluwer, Nikki Jeannotte, Carole Sudhalter
Yogic Heart Publishing logo: Andrea Palframan
Cover concept: Lisa M. Cherry

Cover and Interior Graphics explanation: The cover depicts the blossoming of the yogic heart over a wavy, yellow silk scarf (which some may perceive as sand, since lotuses bloom unscathed from the mud). The interior pages preceding the stories display the same scarf, this time representing ocean waves for the "ocean of yoga" a term coined by Paramahansa Yogananda.

Disclaimer: Although each of the stories in this book are true, please see your doctor rather than taking the authors' journeys as medical advice in any form.

Quotations: Those preceding each story have been gathered by the editor for inspiration over many years, and may vary slightly from their original sources. The words of yogis long-gone have been translated by various scholars over the millenia.

Publisher's Note: While the publisher has made every effort to provide for accuracy in the text at the time of publication, neither the publisher nor the editor can assume responsibility for every error or change that may occur during the printing process or after publication.

Yoga teachers are invited and encouraged to read stories straight from the book in class.

ISBN: 978-0-9813627-0-0
1. Yoga 2. Self-Help 3. Spirituality 4. Inspiration

This book is proudly printed on 100% recycled paper
Printed and bound in Canada ⊕

In memory of Maya Hoffman, Nikki Jeannotte, Aunt Ray, Lou Birenbaum, and my unconditionally-loving grandmothers.

May their next lives be filled with yoga and the great joy, health, and inner peace it brings.

Also dedicated to my mother who recognized my deep, spiritual inclinations early and led me to many leading teachers and teachings of consciousness, to Dr. James D'Adamo ND who beckoned me to the ocean of yoga many moons ago, and to the spirits of Yogananda, Krishnamarcharya, and Vanda Scaravelli whose wisdom inspires me daily.

Contents

Introduction

The yogic heart is one of deep compassion, introspection, awareness, and a feeling of oneness with nature and humanity as a whole. I have been blessed over the past six years to meet a group of dedicated and brave yogic writers who not only emulated such qualities but who have shared with me the most precious and intimate stories of how yoga transformed their lives, welcoming me into their yogic hearts.

Yoga can radically change lives, but it is not an easy task to get many to bare personal stories such as the deep impact yoga had on the core of their existence, on the core of their being. The personal healing that comes through yoga is often beyond words and sometimes beyond the comfort to tell another soul, but the desire of these writers to help others surpassed their apprehension and lit their way.

I created this project during the early years of my multiple chemical sensitivities while struggling with the extreme brain fog that accompanies this illness. Yoga was new in my life and was saving my sanity, but I still craved reading others' transformational stories as they gave me great hope for lasting happiness and health. Realizing that I may be able to help others as well, I reached out to yogis around the world, to collect stories that would daily inspire us all. As I read dozens of peoples' phenomenal yoga journeys, I was mesmerized by the accounts of how yoga had helped many a soul transcend the adversities of much. With gratitude, I can now share these stories with *you*.

In this light, I cannot thank each of the writers enough. Their patience during my several rounds of editing perhaps the most important story of their life exemplifies the great soulfulness which is developed through a focused yogic practice. They will forever be embraced in my heart, along with the following angels who entered my life and helped me manifest this book for all...

Ayu, my Golden Retriever guru, who I woke up to each morning and took for exhilarating walks along the starfish-laden beach. Her incessant barking, should I become lost in thought rather than throw rocks for her to fetch in the ocean, always kept me in the present moment.

Electa Taylor, a 96 year-old friend and yogini in her own right, whose outlook and support ever sustained me.

Davida Elizabeth DeMonte and her sister, Elana Maggal, for helping me contact their uncle, Rabbi Joseph Gelberman, for his story, Reema Datta and Davida for interviewing him for me in New York, Carole Sudhalter for her quick and thorough transcription, and Joshua Greene for sending me his video, *Living Yoga,* for my additional research into the rabbi's background. Eternal gratitude to the late rabbi for giving of his valuable time in his 97th year, and believing in this project as much as we did.

Dave Henry, one of my sage interior-layout artists, Andrea

Palframan, Blanca Camacho and Jennifer Coghill (Indesign, Photoshop and Illustrator experts!) who helped me finish the final interior and exterior layout at the eleventh hour, Christina Heinemann for her front cover font and layout advice, John Miller, my tenacious copyeditor, who went above the call of duty, and Lorraine Gane for her extra copyediting expertise. Plus, the photo expertise of Tom Richardson who shot the front cover's "dancing" mala heart, and of Charles Buchwald whose photo of the yellow silk scarf is thread throughout this book.

And, there were so many more, including...

Melody Poirier who may possibly be the best self-publishing consultant in Canada, for her unflagging support and ideas.

Nikki Jeannotte, one of my incredible transcribers, who I can envision proudly reading the manifestation of her work from above, and the incredible Carole Sudhalter who entered my life as my next talented transcriber when I needed her most.

The renowned Amy Sky and Dharma Mittra, for generously donating Amy's apropos song, *Do You Dance,* and Dharma's stunning *Om* chant for my website. And, the late Jane Hooper whose profoundly-heartfelt poem, *Coming Home,* so encapsulates for me the essence of yoga that it lovingly introduces this book.

A book whose journey was beautified by retreat centers which were havens for my health: Omega Institute, Hollyhock, Poet's Cove, The Dragonfly Ranch, and the Maui Spa Retreat. And made smoother by my dear friends Nancy Anjali Weiser, Beth McDermott, and Linda Markowsly who patiently proofread my final drafts, and Tiffany Estreicher, for expert font advice.

For help in reaching the renowned yogis on the cover, I send immense thanks to Adair Curtis and Florence Eichin for their help with Russell Simmons; Carol Christiansen for her help with Amy Weintraub; Terri Hinte for setting up my interview with Sonny Rollins, and Lydia Zelaya for granting the use of Mariel Hemingway's story. Many thanks, as well, to Alisa DeRosa, Dave Sandford, Kathy Schenker, Joseph Brenner, Sharon Gannon and Sonya Guardo for their helping me attain Sting's story. And, a dozen roses to Reiterations Greeting Cards for their profoundly beautiful greeting cards they donated for me to invite all.

Eternal gratitude also goes to Adina of Salt Spring Books, Sherri of Watermark Books, Michael of Tofino's Mermaid Tales Bookshop, Celeste Mallett, Oona McQuat, Ellen Karpinski, Cindy Sigesmund, Dorothy Price, Mitra Sen, and Monica and Tama of Esther Myers Yoga Studio, for helping me sort through numerous cover designs. And, to West Coast Dharma, whose weekend Vancouver meditation retreats soothed my soul.

Lastly, to the many beautiful souls who have taught me much either in my waking life or in the dreams of my nights: Yogananda, Sivananda, Buddha, Ram Dass, Nichiren Daishonin, Ben, Gem, Thich Nhat Hanh, my many guides, and the two main Debras of my life. And to my great naturopaths, Dr.'s Medrek and D'Adamo, who have saved my body and soul several times.

May you, the reader, find great inspiration in the stories brought to you through this phenomenal web, and may you find true happiness in the ultimate life...

A life filled with yoga.

Preface

Imagine you are walking along a trail in the woods, and out from the evergreens steps an elderly wizard. He appears to be the typical kind, wearing a tall pointy hat, a long grey beard, and a flowing cape. And, he brandishes a golden wand.

He approaches you, gazes deeply into your eyes, and asks, "What is it you'd like most in your life?" And, as in most wizardly fairy tales, he grants you three wishes.

While you'd love the latest cell phone or computer, in your deepest inner wisdom and years of experience on this earthly plane, you know such things materialistic haven't brought you ultimate happiness, so you ask for something you've secretly desired for lifetimes, "I long for inner peace, clarity, and a feeling of oneness with all."

The wizard's wizened face softens into a smile and he glances at your heart, pointing his wand toward the centre of your chest.

"There is an ancient practice called yoga. It has transformed the lives of millions since time immemorial, and it can do so for you. Do yoga every day," suggests this atypical wizard. Then he disappears back into the woods, never to be seen again.

Would you heed the wizard's words? Or, would you assume he was just a figment of your imagination or a crazed old hippie living amongst the tall trees? But, alas, his advice did ring true, as you'd heard much good about yoga — that it calms the mind, allows us to hear our inner voice, and reduces one's reactivity to the turmoil of life. Plus helps us feel oneness with all.

Yet, your mind takes over: *Sounds like a tall promise...almost unbelievable...the stuff of fables,* it says, telling you that you're not flexible enough, not slim enough, perhaps not even young or healthy enough to do yoga. Much advertising hype has given you this impression. But you decide to try yoga anyway, to experience it first-hand, to discover the truth for yourself.

The yogic writers in this book ventured into such territory many years ago, and, through their stories of transformation, you may glean much: inspiration, hope, and an expanded view of reality.

Their stories may be taken as an invitation to yoga and, should you so choose, an invitation to a renewed life. A renewed life that you, one day, may also wish to write about.

Read, reflect, and begin to write the story of *your* beautiful, magical, incredible yogic journey.

With much metta,
Lisa Miriam Cherry
Salt Spring Island, Canada

Please Come Home

Please come home. Please come home.
Find the place where your feet know where to walk
And follow your own trail home.

Please come home. Please come home into your own body,
Your own vessel, your own earth.
Please come home into each and every cell,
And fully into the space that surrounds you.

Please come home. Please come home to trusting yourself,
And your instincts and your ways and your knowings,
And even the particular quirks of your personality.
Please come home.

Please come home.
And once you are firmly there,
Please stay awhile and come to a deep rest within.
Please treasure your home. Please love and embrace your home.
Please get a deep, deep sense of what it's like to be truly home.

Please come home. Please come home.
And when you're really, really ready,
And there's a detectable urge on the outbreath, then
Please come out.

Please come home and please come forward.
Please express who you are to us, and please trust us
To see you and hear you and touch you
And recognize you as best we can.

Please come home. Please come home and let us know
All the nooks and crannies that are calling to be seen.
Please come home, and let us know the More
That is there that wants to come out.

Please come home. Please come home.
For you belong here now. You belong among us.
Please inhabit your place fully so we can learn from you,
From your voice and your ways and your presence.

Please come home. Please come home.
And when you feel yourself home, please welcome us too,
For we too forget that we belong and are welcome,
And that we are called to express fully who we are.
May we wake up and remember who we truly are.

Please come home.
Please come home.
Please come home.

—Jane Hooper

You find yourself in beauty,
unexpectedly absorbed by beauty.
~ Vanda Scaravelli

Blissology 101

Wade Imre Morissette

Had I been born in the early 1960s, you would have found me at Woodstock, gawking at Swami Satchidananda as he did the opening speech or doing headstands at Ram Dass's farm.

Instead, while growing up a decade later, in Ottawa, the chilly capital of Canada, I was your usual kid who loved music, played sports and had a normal upbringing. But, in the back of my mind, I always thought, "There's something more than all this," and after my high school graduation, I discovered there truly was.

I traveled throughout the South Pacific to Australia, New Zealand, Fiji and Hawaii, and my world opened up. Traveling gave me the opportunity to get out of the whole rat race and everybody telling me what I *needed* to do. In New Zealand, when I saw a few guys playing guitar at an airport in Auckland, I thought, *"I'm going to be a guitar player,"* and proceeded to write my first song a few months later. It was the first time I had space to reflect and to think about who I was, where I was going, and to delve into music. I had no idea how fortuitous my lyric "who has awakened me" would be years down the road.

But I was young, convention beckoned, and, after this initial journey, I found myself at the University of Western Ontario, a few hours west of Toronto. When I got there, I had all the intentions of getting into environmental law — until I picked up a book called *The Mystic Path to Cosmic Power,* by Vernon Howard.

The book talked about God and how to connect with Spirit. *That* interested me the most. Could a more spiritually-conscious life allow me to feel more peace, joy and happiness? In search of the answer, I also found insightful books by Jack Kerouac and others on Eastern mysticism and shamanism. As soon as I picked up one, it referred me to another.

Then I found a live mentor.

While at university, I had a Filipino roommate who was in his late thirties, and we lived off campus. He was studying to be a librarian, but he was very much into the spiritual and meditated daily.

So, I ended up at the university *pretending* to study toward environmental law, then I'd come home to this guy I'd befriended who was giving me a bunch of spiritual books. I literally read over thirty books in four months — I'd read from ten at night until four in the morning, sleep until noon, go to a class, leave halfway through that class, and read again!

By the term's end, I decided, *"I can't handle school anymore,"* and at Christmas, when I returned home, told my parents, "Mom, Dad, I've got one course left — I've dropped everything else. You may see me back home in three weeks." Sure enough, two weeks later, I was back in Ottawa having fully dropped out. That must have been the quickest university career ever!

Of course, my friends and classmates from Ottawa and out West started asking "Wade what are you doing? Are you crazy?" I'd reply, "No, I'm just following my heart."

I was looking for *something,* and between reading tons of books on Eastern mysticism and philosophies like Buddhism, I realized, "I'd love to practice this somehow." I yearned for inner peace and composure, but I needed a daily spiritual discipline. Taoist tai chi was too gentle for me, karate too rough, and yoga still hadn't entered my life in a big way.

One morning, a few months after moving to the mountains and ocean off of Vancouver, I woke up and thought: "I have to go to India!" I have no idea why! I'd loved the two or three yoga classes I'd taken in California, but that wasn't much to judge by; yet, I quit my job at the health food store and flew to Chennai.

With that first trip to India, my life shifted again. Backpacking all over the country and up into Nepal on my own with my little guitar, I got hooked on everything — the religion of Hinduism, the lifestyle, and, of course, yoga.

At one point, I became a sannyasin (Sanskrit for *spiritual seeker*) while living at the Osho Ashram and meditating for six hours a day. Back then, because I was young and everything seemed so much more dramatic, when wondrous experiences occurred, I'd think, *"wow, what just happened to me? This is real and this is something I'd like to pursue!"* The time I was sitting in a chair doing Kundalini practices and felt a "current" zip through my body, jerking me right onto the floor, was just one example.

In retrospect, fifteen years later, I now know that I was probably just having energetic releases because of my intense meditation practice. As my practice grew stronger, however, and after many more hours of meditation, I realized that yoga was more than just performing a series of physical postures — with meditation being the final key to transformation.

Returning home after my first trip to India, I was hooked. All I wanted was to become a dedicated yogi and, for the next five years, I traveled back and forth between India and Vancouver regularly. At ashrams, there were always people who wanted to talk about energy and consciousness. India was a place that validated everything I thought.

~ ~ ~

Yoga became a way for me to connect with God and Spirit while living in the world. Just by being true to my practice and doing an hour and a half of asanas, pranayama, and chanting each day, I'd feel centered and calm, balanced and grounded, powerful and humble. Much less stressed and much more connected, I'd feel really high and feel very deeply God's spirit. It seemed like the perfect balance between karate and tai chi — I could be really mindful and receptive in my practice, but, if I so desired, be really vigorous too.

I thrived on such great bliss but, as I matured and got married, it was less about always looking for these deeper experiences and more about having a *steady*, integrated connection while performing my daily activities: paying taxes, changing diapers, going to work, and cleaning the dishes. These also required inner peace and focus, a steady flow and rhythm of connection, and can become blissful in themselves.

I became more aware of the shadow aspects of myself, such as my tendency to worry and to be out of the present moment if I don't do my practice regularly. When I'm not connected to my inner being, that's when I'm less compassionate; that's when I fear; that's when I worry; that's when I mistrust, and that's when I run away from intimacy. Yoga helps me face these aspects of myself and move on.

I strive to be constantly aware so that any time when I choose a thought that's not love or a thought where I beat myself up or judge other people in a negative way, I can choose something different. This I consider self-empowerment, which is the *real*, daily path to enlightenment. It's not like I'm cured of all my negative patterns because of yoga, but yoga lets me see that I have the *choice* to choose either the positive or negative — the choice of which path I want to take.

~ ~ ~

As a boy, I used to go to church and would hold a candle beside the priest while he gave his sermon. I remember staring at the flame and it seeming really peaceful.

Now I realize that I was actually meditating — I was actually practicing yoga and didn't even know it. It all just developed one step at a time.

Our daily environment often removes us from Spirit, but when my mind is calm and focused, I'm in the perfect environment. It can arise just by my sitting on a cushion with my eyes closed, by watching my breath, watching a flame, by chanting, or by any other meditation or asana on which I choose to focus my mind.

My dream, so many years ago, was to experience a bliss-like joy — that real, rooted "God-joy" where one feels incredibly connected.

My wish came true. I followed my heart and yoga was the way to go.

Reflections

At the center of your being, you have the answer.
You know who you are and you know what you want...
Abide at the center of your being.
~ Lau Tzu

My Yogic Blessing

Mariel Hemingway

I am thinking about control today. How hard I have worked to get some feeling of control in my life! Most of the people in my family seemed to be at the mercy of uncontrollable and unhappy forces, so I never wanted to let changes just happen to me. I didn't trust life.

Clutching hard to make my body and mind do what I thought I wanted, I made myself physically sick and pushed my emotions to the brink of collapse. It wasn't until I began to learn about surrender that I started to change some of my unhealthy patterns. Warrior I pose is a good one for me because it mimics the stance of the great warrior, Arjuna, as he surrendered his ego and sense of separation from all beings. That is something I always have to work on.

My obsessive behavior is cut from the same cloth as all the other addictive substance abuse tendencies in my family. We Hemingways are (always) trying to find an easy way out of the pain and disappointment life serves up.

I traveled from one want to the next, seeking comfort and joy in winning acting roles and the love of my peers or even things as trivial as a silk carpet or the perfect physique. I was looking in all the wrong places. Real beauty does not come from the full dynamics of a complex posture, just as it does not come from great bone structure, silicone or the accolades of playing a marvelous role in a movie.

~ ~ ~

I first started meditating after discovering I was pregnant with (my first daughter) Dree. I was reading all kinds of research on how the fetus responds to practically everything in the mother's world, so I assumed that the calming effect of meditation would be beneficial for both of us.

I began with a guided meditation called *Opening to Receive*, which taught me to invite in and receive love and anything else I needed at the time. After about a year of working with the tape, I had the confidence to simply meditate with gentle music in the background. That was the same time period when my hatha yoga practice was evolving to more conscious breath and body movements.

Gradually, I discovered that the concentration on breathing during class helped me focus into a rewarding meditation if I continued to sit after the active movements were over. It's a natural progression from vigorous movement to stillness and silence.

The next sign on my path was pointed out by Dr. Peter

Evans, my spiritual teacher (and doctor). I said that he seemed to be a person who meditates, and when he acknowledged that he did, I asked for instruction (on the type of meditation he practiced). He told me that he couldn't teach me, but asked if I had read *Autobiography of a Yogi*, the story of the enlightened Indian master, Paramahansa Yogananda, who played a leading role in introducing yoga to the West before his death in 1952.

To put it bluntly, I was mesmerized by *Autobiography of a Yogi*. At first, I learned the meditation basics I'd been lacking, like how to start and what to focus on. None of the techniques was terribly difficult, but my ability to go deeply inside naturally increased with the time I put into silent practice. The glimpses of bliss I had were more real than any gift I ever received.

~ ~ ~

One of the nicest aspects I've developed from my yoga practice is to laugh at myself. I come from a family where conversation was either purely surface (what wine shall we have with the trout?) or purely caustic (are you even going to taste the food before you turn it into a salt mine?). Far from being a judgmental competition, yoga can sometimes be a celebration of humor. Accepting that fact is my path to more understanding and joy.

I want to reach an inner stillness that leads me to peace, because when I am truly peaceful, I'm sometimes able to reach beyond to connect with a sense of unconditional love — God's eternal joy. Yoga brings feelings of breathless love for me. I raise my spine, lifting it until it contracts and slightly constricts my breath. When I release, there's a rush of exhilaration that fills my body. It feels very pure to me, reminding me that love is universal, unconditional, belonging to us all.

In my yoga and even more important, in my meditation, I find endless, unfading joy that comes from God and spirit. It envelops me.

~ ~ ~

The awful tragedy of (my older sister) Margaux's death, in 1996, came out of nowhere. She was as healthy as she had been in years, and her life was looking up. Our relationship had regained a trust and openness that we had lost. It was better than ever. We had visited together in Idaho a few months before, sharing some very sweet insights. We laughed and cried over the way we had played the complementary roles of rebel and good girl in order to survive in our strange family.

I plunged into a state of emotional confusion after her death. Margaux was central to my definition of myself. She was not the person I wanted to be, but we shared too many things for me not to identify with her. I was a little girl, looking carefully through big eyes, when she began being wild and also having her success. That may be why detachment and observation in my practice, and often in my life, come naturally to me.

The coroner released a sensational report finding that her death was a suicide. This prompted national headlines about "The Curse of the Hemingway Family." I was wounded and angry. The last thing I needed was to be told that I am part of an incurably sick and damned family.

Instead of feeling more like Mariel, able to distinguish myself from my sister, I became more confused about my own identity. I had always struggled to be myself, not Margaux — I wanted not to be as big as she was; I wanted to be known as the actress, not the model; I wanted to be the healthy one, not the alcoholic and drug addict.

But when she died, instead of feeling that she was gone, I felt I really was her. I feared I would have to become the sick person who lived inside me, carrying on the family curse. It was in my genes and in my destiny. Somehow, I didn't go crazy, even with all my biggest fears dancing in my head. I tried to use my meditation like a blanket from the cold, lost in my belief in God.

It was at this time that I realized the value of simply continuing my practice. While my sessions were definitely not inspired, they were organized and precise. I had difficulty with full, rich breaths and my sense of observation was not in tune, but I kept practicing. The asana work calmed my body, allowing me to sit in meditation.

Since the thoughts trying to overwhelm me were so powerful, I made my physical yoga practice very vigorous. The harder I worked physically, the easier my meditation became. I gradually began to let go of my fear of Margaux's karma, realizing that her pain and problems were hers and not mine.

Dr. Evans looked at me one day and said, "Mariel, you are not your sister."

He somehow understood how deeply I needed to hear those words from a trusted friend, and those simple words released me. Slowly, I reoccupied my own body in Ketchum, Idaho, with two young daughters and a husband. I could breathe again.

On good days, creating this centeredness can be the most challenging part of my yoga practice. Subtle yet specific waves of energy awaken in my body. It's almost as though I can feel my stagnant blood beginning to course and flow, like sand slowly pouring through the waist of an hourglass. The tightness begins to ease. Breathing deeply and consciously, I feel connected to energy and my heart begins to beat faster. It is nice to listen to my body and to feel in control of at least this one thing.

~ ~ ~

In November of 2001, I bundled up our little Crisman-Hemingway clan and headed to the island of Kauai for a combined celebration of Thanksgiving and my 40th birthday. The day seemed important beyond the mere turning of a calendar page.

Somehow, I felt this birthday represented a subtle transition in my lifelong quest to understand myself. Rather than trying to figure out who I am, I am learning to accept the person that I now understand myself to be.

Surrender is far more than just a little mini vacation I give myself. Like the deaths we deal with — of habit, youth, changing friendships, joys gone by, our loved ones — life is the practice of surrender. My life is constantly guiding me to learn to give in to what is happening around me, to accept my circumstances, accept my choices, and especially to surrender to the shocks life deals me.

I'm beginning to feel that I have some things to show for my efforts. I have finally found a way to eat that suits me, my hatha yoga exercises my body, heart, and mind, and it isn't an overstatement to say that I love the practice.

My dependence on "acting" as a means of self-definition has diminished, and I no longer feel a helpless victim of my family's strange interactions and flawed genetic pool.

Being Mariel is all right by me.

Live each present moment completely,
and the future will take care of itself.
~ Paramahansa Yogananda

Sarina's Gift

Manuela Rohr

Sarina was born four months early by emergency C-section, weighing only one pound and fifteen ounces.

My husband and I had just celebrated our second anniversary a week before, and the baby had made its first move, kicking my belly for both of us to feel. We were ecstatic. As this was my fourth pregnancy, my husband and I knew with absolute certainty that this time we would have a child who would live.

Little did we know, we were expecting a premature baby — a *high risk* preemie.

When my water broke, my husband rushed me to the hospital. The grave look on my doctor's face destroyed any hope we had that we could fix what was happening. For eight hours, I was monitored, hoping for the miracle of keeping my baby safe inside.

At 8 pm, her heart stopped beating. Alarms sounded wildly. In a frenzy of doctors and nurses rushing me to the operating room, I caught a glimpse of my husband's startled eyes. My body was shaking violently. The deep pain and sorrow in his face reached down to my bones.

"Breathe, breathe for your baby," an inner voice told me. At first, I was unable to follow it. I had lost control.

~ ~ ~

As I grew up, things came easily to me. By nature, I was athletic; no tree was too high, no distance too far. I studied to become a gymnastic teacher and pushed through everything, holding tight, ever my way.

But I was hungry for something different. I knew that there was more to life, more than always pushing my edge, and that "something deeper" was deeper inside of me. As grace would have it, my father bought me my first yoga book. It talked about the balance between the body and the mind. Soon, I started practicing on my own and signed up for a class.

Being mindful of my body was new to me. In yoga, however, while connecting to my breath, a great stillness and feeling of being in the present moment enveloped me and I realized there was so much more.

~ ~ ~

Immediately after my baby girl's birth, she was intubated, a respirator breathing for her. As her lungs had not yet developed, she had a very small chance to survive.

I'd listen to the doctor talking about the dangers she faced. I can still hear his words. Back then, I was unable to make sense of what they meant. In my recollection, I tell myself to breathe, but my mouth is dry and I can't find my voice. I feel tears roll down my cheeks, then I watch the doctor walk away. A grave silence drapes its weight over my body like a heavy blanket. Every muscle shrinks and my senses are numbed.

"What is happening?" I wonder, believing I've lost my baby, feeling like my heart is torn apart. For what feels like an eternity, I escape into a deep cloud of unsafe stillness. I feel so alone.

The sounds of the Neonatal Intensive Care Unit (NICU) lure me back. My body hurts and my breasts have started to swell, ready to feed my baby. As if in playback mode, the doctor's voice repeats itself: "If she survives, she may have multiple handicaps. She may never be able to breathe on her own."

I finally open my eyes, and realize that I am not alone. No matter how hard I try to ignore it, the incubator in front of me is real. Breathing deeply, I try to soften my shoulders and to let go of the grip at my heart. I plead with my mind to keep me in the present moment, and I beg the universe to please keep my baby alive.

I yearn to touch her, to hold her in my arms, but I remember that I must ask for permission first. "The baby needs to be stable before being touched," the doctor had instructed me. For two days, I ache to see my child. Instead, because of the big scar from my C-section, I have to stay in bed waiting for my healing to begin. All I have is the Polaroid my husband brought me in his worried state, showing me the tiniest baby I have ever seen.

I sit there, trying to understand. The sign on the left hand corner of the incubator reads *"Sarina"* in beautiful, handwritten letters, with a border of pink hearts all around. A voice breaks into the fog of my mind: "Hi, I am Pam, your primary nurse. I made the sign for your daughter. I met your husband last night and he told me what he'd like your daughter's name to be: *Sarina*. He says it means *little princess*." I listen, still unable to speak in my traumatized state.

"Your daughter is beautiful, do you want to touch her?" she asks. I can't understand what she means by "beautiful." She opens a small round window and lets me reach inside. I have finally received *permission*. I gently reach through the incubator window and, with my forefinger, barely touch Sarina's fragile arm. It is the only safe spot to touch on her tiny body, the rest being covered with a mess of wires and tubes. Her eyes are closed, her thumb in her mouth, her arm and my finger appear the same size.

Suddenly, my maternal instinct breaks through as I bond with my baby through the incubator wall, feeling her paper-thin skin. *She needs me, I need to be strong. I need to breathe for her.*

"Slow and deep inhalation, calm and quiet exhalation," my inner voice instructs.

Being able to connect with my breath saves me from getting further swept away by the turmoil swirling within — a key teaching I'd learned on the yoga mat. My breath connects me to my mind, and my breath connects me to my child, keeping me from falling apart.

I needed to stay with this unpleasant experience, as a calm

witness to it all. I would have loved to speed things up, to rush to the finish line; yoga taught me, rather, to stay present with the ride.

~ ~ ~

I didn't know, back then, of all the complications and setbacks that would come our way. I couldn't imagine that it would take months until we could bring our daughter home. I couldn't let the thought come close to me that she could die even though I knew she might; her handicaps might be too severe to keep her alive or we might even be asked if we want her to live or to die. What I knew for sure was that I needed to practice living with her, moment to moment. The present moment was all I had.

As the days went by, I observed the tragedies unfolding around us. I saw parents's faces pale with grief. A mother next to me wept helplessly because she learned her baby will be blind. Alarm overwhelmed me with thoughts of all the unknown that could take our daughter's life.

Slowly, I learned to live with uncertainty. For several months, I lived at the hospital each day and many nights. I bonded with my child through her incubator wall and felt her body connect with mine. As she could not breathe on her own, I breathed *for* her. Slowly and deeply, I inhaled; calmly and quietly, I exhaled. I felt life's energy — *prana* — flow through my own body and offered it to my daughter's seemingly lifeless one. I would share my life's energy to replenish the life I had birthed.

My most basic desire — to stabilize this chaos — loosened

its grip. I realized it was beyond my power. Nothing ever remains the same; everything moves, everything changes. I realized that it's the *holding on*, the *attachment* that hurts the most, not the letting go.

~ ~ ~

Sarina was a strong fighter. She came home after six months in the NICU, remained on oxygen, and needed it for two more years. "By school age, preemies catch up," I was told. That never happened. Being deprived of oxygen in her early years may be the cause.

Our life has been full of overwhelming obstacles. It has also been blessed with new beginnings and the magical force of learning to trust and surrender. Sarina was thirty months old when she took her first step, thirty-six months when she first spoke. At 10 years of age, she wrote her first letters. This year, at 17, she gave herself — and us — the gift of being able to ride her bike.

Her love for and her gift of language — both in English and German — startles us and make us smile every day. At times, she doesn't find her voice easily, but she adds her spark to simple things: "One water with a cherry, please," being both glamorous and deeply unpretentious at the same time.

She sees beauty where our own eyes turn away, and dreams of perhaps becoming a nurse, a doctor or an artist. She dreams about having her own loving husband and the children she might have. It's up to something bigger than us that it should happen.

~ ~ ~

On my yoga mat, I had learned to practice self-reflection and clearly saw the habits that didn't serve me well. I learned to pay attention to when I was pushing too hard and to accept what my body was able to do in the present moment. It was the quality of "letting go" that I needed most. I learned to trust that when I approach an edge and let go, I won't be lost. Perhaps I will even fly; there is something bigger than "me" holding me.

Sitting by the incubator was the most difficult posture that I ever had to hold, but it held an unforeseen blessing: in the midst of the unfolding drama of Sarina's birth and life, I was able to bring what I learned on my yoga mat, so many years ago, into her life.

Dealing with the day-by-day challenges of a special child allows me to stay present, to be open to whichever posture I choose, to be able to walk gracefully into the mystery of each moment.

Next to her life, these are the most precious gifts that I have ever received.

I do not understand the mystery of grace — only that it meets
us where we are, but does not leave us where it found us.
~ Anne LaMott

Absent No More

Rosanne Harrison

For many years, as I was growing up, I was under the impression that I knew a lot about everything. By the time I was 18 years old, I was a recovering drug addict and college drop-out. It was December, 1993, and I sat alone in a rehab center wearing a long sleeve sweatshirt and sweatpants because my body was so itchy from the drugs releasing from my system. But I was okay, these were my choices, and no one was going to get me to apologize for any of it.

My new choice was to get sober and finish college, and that's what I did. I bulldozed my way through life again, but this time I set my intentions on a healthy one instead of a life filled with night creatures. I went back to school, stayed sober, found love, and was married by the age of 21. I thought that I knew it all and that I had it all. Little did I know that I really didn't know much of anything.

Fortunately, something powerful would come along to awaken me. And to help me deal with the pain of my past.

~ ~ ~

To those on the outside, my childhood may have appeared ideal. I grew up with a very health-conscious mother who put me in meditation classes when I was eight and in aerobics classes most of my life. I hated all of it — I was a tomboy. I liked swimming, running and climbing trees. I *needed* to be rough because that was the only way I knew how to survive. Survive in a paradox, that is.

You see, my parents loved to beat each other, and my brother and I became part of the circle. As a teenager, the last thing I wanted to do was to sit quietly and feel the heaviness in my soul, but I did. It was there and drugs were my only option. Drugs quieted my mind; they were my maya, and I loved them.

When I got married, that all felt like a lifetime ago. My husband was sober, as was I, and together we "had the world at our fingertips." At 21, I still needed to be needed, and he needed me. It was a perfect match. We became each other's drug, but at least it was legal.

We lived in Denver, Colorado where my son was born and I continued with college, graduating with a degree in English. All my life, I'd put so much weight into being educated because no one in my family had ever gone to college — I was to be the first. Every ounce of my essence went into getting that degree. But once I graduated, I thought, *"Now what?"*

I recall waking up the day after my graduation ceremony not feeling any happier, and realizing that nothing had changed. Nothing had changed because *I* hadn't changed. I saw that everything I held with such high regard — degrees, money, being the perfect partner — was just an illusion; these things didn't touch my core and I couldn't accept them anymore.

But my "awakening" had been many months in the making. During my pregnancy I had developed sciatica, and my doctor advised me to lie on my bed with the upper half of my body hanging upside down and to swim, as well. But when I passed by an Iyengar yoga class at the gym one day and saw everyone doing headstands, I thought, *"That beats lying on my bed!"* and started practicing yoga that morning.

My eyes widened that day because of yoga and I hated yoga for that. I didn't know if I was ready to wake up and I was terrified of the possibilities. I was actually more afraid of the *joy* that my life could have than I was of the consequences of changing; it was the light that petrified me, not my shadows.

~ ~ ~

We moved to Chicago in 2000, and I immediately began practicing at another yoga studio. A year later, I found myself in Ana Forrest's teacher training. I don't know how I got there other than divine intervention. I hated the first class; in fact, I hated most of the classes. I was a bull, I wouldn't surrender, and I wouldn't cry. I wouldn't give in to my soul, which just wanted some safe space and some room to "just be."

Then September 11th happened. Ana made us come back after our break to chant and meditate. I am so grateful that she did. I was split wide open and I was absolutely terrified, yet the chanting and meditation made me feel stronger in some strange way. It was an inner strength that I'd always told everyone that I had, but never genuinely felt; I'd shown a rough demeanor to the world because I feared being vulnerable — I feared being myself. Now my truth was more powerful than my illusion.

~ ~ ~

I never wanted to teach anything, let alone yoga. I had been a writer and editor up until my yoga training, but something called me to teach. I finished my certification, divorced my husband, and taught yoga all over Chicago for the next three years. Whenever I doubted myself or questioned my motives, a student would thank me for the class. One of the students pulled me aside a couple weeks after giving birth and, through tears, told me that I am part of the reason why her son is on this Earth. These are the reasons that I teach yoga.

Teaching yoga was the first time in my life that I felt I could give a part of myself away and, instead of feeling empty, feeling abundance and joy. But it was no longer about me. It was about being present in my own life so that I could be present in someone else's. I saw that everything matters and that nothing should ever be discounted if it comes from a place of truth and honest intentions.

When I began teaching English at a high school on Chicago's west side, my yoga came with me. Every Tuesday, after school, I ran a yoga club. It started small, but then more students — as well as teachers — started showing up every week. The students balked at first, as all teenagers would, then one of them opened up. "This is the first time in my life that I feel peace in my mind," she whispered.

Two weeks later, during a hip-opening class, another student released. I just leaned in and told her that I knew what she was feeling — that I've been there, and to just feel it, to be present. She was, and even though the tears fell, I knew that when she left my class her gentle strength was beginning to awaken within. I love teaching teenagers.

I love that, today, I can offer someone my time, and walk away feeling like I've received a blessing. I love that today I feel lighter when I listen to someone's story. I love that I can teach a pose or put my hand on someone who is suffering and see their eyes light up because, just for that brief moment, they know that they matter to another human being; they see that we are connected in some way beyond this world of maya.

I have exhausted my soul in the pursuit of knowledge and I was never happy, I have used knowledge as a way to ostracize people from my life, I have used my experiences as a drug addict to frighten people or to intimidate them, and I have used my "awesome intellect" to prove my "superiority" to others. All because, in reality, I felt insecure. What came of all this chaos in my mind, however, was just self-imposed separation and suffering. I like how, today, I know that I don't know much.

Today, through moments, I can feel peace and love. I just pause and remember that I can love completely what I don't completely understand.

With the quality of mindfulness...we see
beyond the surface of life, beyond what we have been taught,
beyond the conventional and assumed.
~ Sharon Salzberg

Finding My Perfect Self

Taz Tagore

During my first yoga class, I nearly cried. Not from inner peace or letting go, but from shame. It was a burning hot yoga class held in Cambridge, Massachusetts, and a few days before I began my graduate studies at Harvard Business School.

My former boyfriend, an accomplished tennis player and marathon runner, had brought me to the class and was practicing a few mats away from me. The heating system was spewing out stale, hot air. And, like creatures of the rainforest, beads of moisture regularly materialized, gathered momentum, and slid down our bodies. But I didn't care.

I was being introduced to yoga at the apex of my achievement and success-oriented way of life; I had spent years posturing and politicking through the upper echelons of student government, graduate school and the corporate world, and I wanted to be challenged in yoga and to conquer any poses taught. Young and competitive, I planned to excel at it all.

As soon as I stepped into the room with my boyfriend, however, I felt tricked — it was full with dancers and athletes whose bodies had been sculpted from years of coaching and performance. Rather embarrassed by my presumption that I'd fit right in, I quickly changed into loose clothing and disappeared into a corner of the room. Not for long though.

Our teacher was like a yogic drill sergeant, quietly confident in his skills and punishing toward those who couldn't keep up. For him, yoga was a path paved with pain and determination. He demanded our best, so I pushed myself hard to find and maintain the "perfect pose."

Looking around at my fellow yogis doing headstands and crow pose, I became curious but also felt a great deal of envy. I desperately tried to keep pace with everyone, inventing ways to cheat and cut corners. Eventually, I just slipped in a pool of my own sweat and fell flat on my belly in plank pose. Self-conscious, I barely made it through the rest of the class.

After class, however, a surge of competitiveness awakened inside of me. "*I will figure out a way to conquer yoga,*" I staunchly decided, and concocted a plan that encompassed running twice a week and a switching to a healthy diet. I was determined to become "the perfect yogini."

Two years later, just a few weeks before graduating from the MBA program at Harvard, I thought I was the model of that yogini: A lithe, limber yoga practitioner, the woman I'd envisioned becoming. "Drill sergeant yoga" had radically transformed my body. Apparently, yoga was also known to transform people's lives, though it certainly hadn't done so with mine.

I still compared my yoga practice to that of others in class, I continued to determine my goals by measuring what others my age had accomplished, and I desperately sought to prove that I was good enough by trying to conquer every task and obstacle in my path. I rarely ever listened to — or even noticed — my voice within.

But my intuition, being honed from all the yoga I'd done, began to assert itself in seemingly strange and unexpected ways. And, with my graduation date looming and no high-powered corporate job lined up, it was a good thing it did. Especially when I heard about a popular ten-day, silent meditation retreat.

"Sounds interesting," I thought, and, instead of balking, actually listened to my inner voice and considered a radical choice: signing up for the next retreat which commenced the day after graduation. Through a combination of both my yoga classes and being blessed with a mystical sister, I'd learned about the benefits of vipassana meditation. And, many yogic friends who'd done the course had sung its praise. I had no idea how to meditate or whether I could survive ten days of silence, but I decided to take the plunge. What choice did I have?

My first day post-graduation, I eagerly drove to the countryside retreat centre, daydreaming of a blissful vacation: *ten days of rest and relaxation in the country.* With a room and food provided, I wouldn't have to do anything but sit around and breathe. Or so I thought..

Countryside it was, good food it was, blissful it was not.

Having to sit down and pay attention to my body for ten hours a day, everyday, required a near-Herculean effort. Instead of meditating, all I wanted to do was start my next job or next project — *anything* to occupy my mind and feel busy. During the first few days, I took mental notes for a new play I planned to write, a new photography series I wanted to shoot, and developed an action plan for my summer vacation; I essentially "worked" during the meditation sessions and secretly wrote out my plans at night.

Eventually, when my idea bank ran out, I decided to actually try meditating. After all, I thought, I could probably master that too. *"It's just a matter of focusing on the techniques,"* I told myself. *"I could do it in half the time of the other attendees!"*

Some time between learning to observe my breath and the sensations on my skull, my inner voice spoke to me again. This time, it was loud and clear.

"You are *COMPLETELY* detached from yourself," it said. "You don't know *who* you are. Everything you do is aimed at pleasing *others*."

It was true. Even though my resume claimed otherwise, I didn't know who I was or what I really wanted in life. I tried ignoring this awful truth that emanated from within, but the voice grew stronger throughout the retreat. It told me that I had actually abused myself in the pursuit of a powerful body and that the *real* purpose of yoga was far deeper than improving one's physique.

As I continued shifting my attention in small, finely tuned

increments from the top of my head to the tip of my toes during the meditation, I realized that yoga could not be mastered like a finance class, but I'd treated it as such; instead of stilling my mind and nurturing my soul, my yoga practice had simply fed my mind and ego. This time, I cried real tears of shame.

~ ~ ~

I returned to Cambridge, Massachusetts a different person. I spent most of my time sitting in meditation, taking long walks, and writing poetry and prose. And, my yoga practice shifted too. I now chose to practice slow, gentle yoga; I stopped doing jump-backs, stopped coveting the perfect handstand, and began to see yoga studios as spaces in which I was good enough just as I was — without my doing or perfectly accomplishing anything.

I now gravitated to a different type of yoga teacher Instead of idolizing those with ethereal bodies and a "superb technique," I sought out teachers who taught me about the *inner* meaning of yoga. One of my favorites was a teacher who often reminded us, "Advanced yoga practitioners are people who are compassionate with themselves and know when to rest in child's pose."

Yoga became a special time for me to listen to my inner voice and heed its wisdom. Sometimes it encouraged me to push my limits, other times it encouraged me to deeply rest. I became overwhelmed with gratitude for my practice, my body, and the gift of life, and began offering quiet thanks with each pose I did.

Slowly, I began to create greater symmetry between my life

both on and off the mat. I began making different choices such as seeking friends and job opportunities in which I connected with others who shared my newfound perspective on the world; I wanted to be surrounded by those who also preferred focusing on the richness of life, not what they didn't have or couldn't get. Joy, gratitude and acceptance became the primary emotional anchors in my life instead of stress, fear, and self-loathing.

In 2005, I took a huge leap of faith and left the corporate world — and my six-figure salary — to start the Reciprocity Foundation, a nonprofit organization dedicated to helping homeless youth break the cycle of poverty through a combination of educational career and wellness-programming involving yoga and more.

When I took that leap of faith, I finally understood the true meaning of yoga: The complete union of spiritual practice with everyday life. Instead of trying to build a powerful body, I decided to wield my *inner* power in ways that would help those in need; along with focusing on "breathing and resting" as part of my new yoga practice, I decided to also add breathing and resting into my daily life; instead of being envious of "better" or stronger yogis, I became content to gaze inward and revel in the beauty of my blossoming yogic heart.

As my yoga practice and my life merge into a single path, I am finally becoming the yogini that I was meant to be.

Reflections

*Love is the only path. It brings unity by
healing the painful split between the body, mind and heart.
When these unite, one merges with the soul like the countless
rivers and streams merge into the vast ocean.*
~ *Swami Kripalu*

Into the Light

Amy Weintraub

November in coastal New England is a time to gather with friends in front of the fire. It's a wonderful month to sit before the computer and finish that assignment, write a long e-mail to a faraway friend or curl up in your favorite chair with a good novel. But if you're feeling depressed, you may not have the energy or the will to do any of these things.

For the sixteen years that I lived there, November in New England was my low point, the time when my chronic depression came into full bloom, fertilized by heavy cloud cover and rain. There were few temptingly warm days to break the bleak monotony of life lived indoors, and dawn broke without a glimpse of the sun.

On just such a damp, gray November afternoon, during the tail end of the hurricane season in 1985, I sat on my psychiatrist's couch feeling a familiar sense of emptiness. I didn't suffer in the way Virginia Woolf made famous, with "wave after wave of agony." Depression for me was, as Emily Dickinson described it, "an element of blank." A stultifying numbness had settled in. Sometimes I rose in the morning with what felt like a layer of cotton batting between my brain and my cranium. Neither coffee nor exercise could penetrate the thickening. I moved as though through a fog. My senses were dulled and my perceptions impaired.

One day, I sent a cheque to the health insurance carrier for the entire chequing account balance instead of the payment due; I forgot important meetings; I lost keys, gloves, and once, even my car in a parking lot.

"You're one of those people who will always have empty pockets," my psychiatrist declared, and I visualized myself, like Virginia Woolf, filling those empty pockets with stones and stepping into the river.

Until I took my first yoga class at Kripalu Center, in Lenox, Massachusetts, I believed that my psychiatrist was right. My empty pockets and my need for antidepressant medication felt like a life sentence. In that first class, the instructor had us place our hands in prayer position in front of our hearts. "Take a deep breath in," she said, "and fill your heart with light. Hold the breath and feel the light as healing energy, expanding through your chest and through your whole body. Exhale and open your palms to receive. Stay empty. God loves your empty hands."

Right there, in that moment, I realized that there was another way to see my depression. "Empty pockets" wasn't a curse, but a blessing. I had more room for the divine inside me. This new insight didn't blow the fog of depression from my mind, it simply opened a window through which I saw the possibility of feeling better, the possibility of extending, through the rest of my day, the good feeling I had in those moments after yoga class. In those moments, I felt alive, not just in my mind, which at that moment was perceiving how good I felt, not just in my heart, expanding with love, but down into my fingertips, up to the crown of my head and down into my toes. Every cell felt awake and in a state of awe, a state beyond happiness in which I felt connected to all beings.

Might it be possible to feel this more in my life, I wondered? To live from this awakened state? After nine months of practicing every day with an audiotape, and two or three more visits to Kripalu as a guest, I had an experience that showed me the potential for living an awakened life.

I was driving in my van, listening to a tape by the well-known psychologist, Jean Houston, who was leading a guided visualization. I was at a red light with my eyes half-closed when Jean asked me to name myself. The light was still red, so I closed my eyes for an instant. Immediately, I was filled with abundance: the feeling of abundance, the word abundance, and the name. As the light turned green, I accelerated, named myself *Abundance,* and laughed out loud. In that moment, my pockets were full!

After that experience, with the guidance of a psychiatrist, I reduced then eliminated my anti-depressant medication over the course of nine months. That was in 1989, and I haven't taken any kind of psychopharmacological agent since. My yoga practice became my medicine. As I did pranayama and kriya throughout my asana practice, I was strengthening the container of my body and clearing out toxins so that my own awakened prana could flow more freely. As I paid attention to sensations in my body through the poses, I was cultivating witness consciousness and became less reactive and more responsive to life's challenges. The old negative self-talk began to dissolve as new neural connections were formed.

I still felt the grief of a relationship that was ending, but there was now a sense of observing it, too. So, when I was in tears, rolling around on my yoga mat, it was as if I was looking down on my crying self. I said, *"Oh, Amy, what a big heart you have,"* because when I was truly depressed and medicated, I was mostly numb to my feelings. As soon as I said those words, I felt an inner smile. I was grieving, but I was aware of a deeper level of joy, untouched by the loss.

I continue to practice every day, but my time on the mat is no longer just my medicine. It is the source of an inner knowing, not only of who I am, but of who you are, who my kitty is, who the hundred and eight year-old cactus on my hike through the Tucson Mountains is. I know that I am not my body, not my present mood, not my accomplishments or my failures. And this knowledge is the source of an abiding serenity and joy that lies beneath the surface of all the challenges life presents.

Yes, I still feel the barbs of life, but, when I practice, clearing the space again every day, there is nothing for them to stick to. They just sail through. Equanimity is present. Presence is present. True abundance to me.

Reflections

Ultimately, it is self-realization that is the true goal of yoga.
~ *Sri Swami Satchidananda*

My Holographic Life

Sting

The middle of the night, somewhere over the north Pacific in the back of a DC-10 at 35, 000 feet…

The plane is empty but for my band, the crew and me — forty tired guys sleeping off too many working nights in a row. Each night a different city, sometimes a different country or even a different continent. None of us has slept in our own bed for months, but nine hours in a DC-10 is as good a place as any to catch up on some sleep.

Only, I'm not sleeping. While my crew and band mates are snoring and dreaming of home, I'm standing on my head between the bulkhead and the empty economy section.

The stewardesses have been giving me strange looks since I began my yoga practice an hour ago. Now, don't get me wrong. I'm as tired as everybody else is. But when I saw that space on the floor, I knew how I wanted to use my time. I wanted to practice yoga.

I can see the full moon out of the little window. I feel the vibrations of the engines through the floor from my head up to my feet. It sounds like OM to the power of six thousand horses. I'm vibrating with it upside down with an inverted smile on my face. This is truly flying.

They say that when the pupil is ready, the teacher will appear. My yoga journey began in 1990. My first teacher, Danny, walked into my studio in London and asked if I wanted to learn about yoga. I had no idea what yoga was, but I was intrigued enough to ask him to show me. Which he did.

I was impressed by both his quiet confidence and the strength and flexibility which he demonstrated. I was even more impressed after I tried to emulate some of his movements.

I had always thought of myself as fit. My job demands it. I was an athlete when I was younger and ran every day. But could I bend forward and lay my palms on the floor with straight legs? No way. Nor could I complete a simple sun salutation without huffing and puffing like an old train. This teacher's breath had been smooth and effortless. I asked him to come to my house the next day and teach me.

Not so coincidentally, my house in London used to belong to Yehudi Menuhin, the violin maestro. It was Mr. Menuhin who first brought the renowned B.K.S. Iyengar, to London in the 1950s to teach yoga. The garden where they practiced daily overlooks a vast park with huge old trees. Menuhin even wrote the foreword to Mr. Iyengar's book, *Light on Yoga*, in 1966.

I feel blessed to practice in that house and partake of the accumulated sadhana, and of their knowledge of and dedication to yoga. I'd like to think that some of their dedication has rubbed off on me, as I have now been practicing yoga six days a week for ten years. And I believe that yoga has provided me with energy and focus that I would not have possessed otherwise.

My work as a performer is physically demanding, and my work as a songwriter challenges my imagination. Yoga has enhanced my capacity in both areas. My duties as a husband and a father, as well as my ability to deal with other relationships, have all been enhanced by a practice that has become inextricably bound to every aspect of my life.

Through yoga, I've sought to know my Self and have managed to gain a number of insights. For example, I now feel that my body carries within it a holographically complete record of everything it has experienced in fifty years. My fears, my prejudices, and my doubts are all somehow reflected in the structure and musculature of my body. Where it is closed and unyielding, resistant to change, I find that I am holding fast to emotional wounds suffered in the past. When I am confident, fearless and open, this too is reflected in the ease with which my body moves.

My yoga practice has given me tools for facing and processing aspects of the unconscious that otherwise could remain hidden and frustrating for a lifetime. It has been a task in my practice of yoga to feel the unlimited aspects of Self as well as to explore and challenge the physical aspects — both pleasant and painful.

This challenge is emotional, intellectual, psychological, physical, and spiritual. I feel that there is an interpenetration between the mind, the body and the spirit of God within. What I think about affects the subtle bodies as well as the physical body and, in turn, the physical functioning affects mind, emotion, intellect, and what I call soul. There is no separation. This I have learned.

I feel a subtle change in the vibration of the airplane. We are starting our descent as the first light of day pierces the eastern horizon. The lights of New Orleans sparkle below us and I give thanks for the new day.

Reflections

My support comes from an internal source so deep
and vast and timeless that it can never be exhausted.
It can never be lost.
~ Rama Berch

A Joyous Refuge

Zo Newell

I was introduced to yoga when I was 14, in 1964. That was the summer after President Kennedy was killed, the summer of the Freedom Riders. Timothy Leary had been kicked out of Harvard but LSD was so uncommon that it was still legal, The Beatles had not yet met the Maharishi, the war in Viet Nam was barely mentioned, and ladies wore gloves and stockings with seams up the back.

At home, my grandmother had died and my mother and I were engaged in mortal combat. She and I could not be under the same roof for too long without one of us (well, me) running into one another's room yelling "I hate you!" and slamming the door thereafter.

My father spent a lot of time off working somewhere, and my brother was temporarily lost to me in a world of sports. I was too young to have a job, too young to do anything, I thought, and anyway, I had no transportation. So I did what many other teenage girls have done in similar circumstances: I declared myself an atheist, wrote poetry, and thought about death.

Sometimes, in our darkest hours, grace appears. Mine appeared in the form of Dr. Rammurti S. Mishra and the community of Ananda Ashram. Also known as Shri Brahmananda Sarasvati, Dr. Mishra was from India and came from a family of meditators and Sanskrit scholars. He was on staff at Bellevue, Manhattan's foremost public psychiatric hospital, and had developed a reputation in the medical community for being able to make progress with difficult, even hopeless-seeming patients, by the (then unheard of) method of teaching them how to meditate. He would work all week at Bellevue, then come up to the ashram on weekends.

One of his students acquired an old estate near Harriman, New York and, in the summer of 1964, was preparing to open its doors as an ashram — a place where people could come study meditation, Sanskrit and yoga. A small core of the doctor's serious students and some other volunteers stayed on the property to renovate it.

Dr. Mishra's book, *Fundamentals of Yoga,* had received some attention and his lectures were very popular in the city, attracting people like my parents who were Quakers and familiar with meditation. (Krishnamurti and Gandhi were two of my father's heroes). But after attending a couple meditation programs at Ananda, my parents found themselves defeated by the length of the programs and the impenetrability of Dr. Mishra's accent.

"I could not understand one word he said!" my mother complained later. However, they met a nice young man who was living there and who wanted to make some money giving guitar lessons. Just the thing for their sulky daughter, mom and dad decided. I learned to play a few chords from Max and, before long, my relieved mother was dropping me off at the ashram in the morning and picking me up in time for supper. I'd hang around all day and tell her that I was helping look after the children of some of the residents.

I do not recall the particular moment I met Dr. Mishra, but I do recall his telling me that *ashram* meant a refuge," and that *ananda* meant joyous refuge. The ashram was both of these for me. I took to meditation and to the sporadic yoga classes with glee. Doctorji's method of teaching hatha yoga to children was to show us a particular pose and say invitingly, "Can you do this?" Physically flexible, I always could.

I trusted him completely. If he suggested that I could do a particular pose, I felt that surely I could, so I was never afraid to try. As he taught, he told stories about the asanas and the ancient yogis who discovered them. He contended that we already knew everything we needed — all the poses were already present inside us, he'd say, along with Sanskrit and the wisdom of the Vedas.

"Feel it!" he'd tell us, over and over. "It is your true nature."

"But what if I don't feel it?" I'd implore.

"It is just maya," he'd affectionately explain, maya being the principle of illusion that tricks us into believing we are something other than eternal and imperishable — the qualities of God. "Omnipotent, omnipresent, omniscient," Doctorji would intone.

Some of the older and more serious meditators viewed me as intrusive, and I can see now that I must have been. My mother would drop me off when it fit her schedule, and the ashram's schedule was flexible at best. Programs lasted for hours with a mix of Sanskrit chanting, a lecture, and meditation. As often as I could, I'd burst cheerfully into the middle of something and rush over to hug Doctorji, whom I regarded as my particular friend.

He always hugged back, then said, "Now go sit down," which I would do, beaming, and stepping carefully amongst the seated meditators. They'd just glare at me or smile back, depending on their feelings about children.

Fourteen is such a vulnerable age. More than anything in my life right then, I needed an adult to tell me that in my innermost, realest nature, I was valuable, eternal and already possessed of all the wisdom of the ages. I needed a *tool* to help me deal with my mother's sorrow, my father's absences, my feeling of being from another planet, and meditation and yoga gave me that.

As I understood it, sitting in meditation and asanas (moving in meditation) were just different aspects of the same process. "Like matter," exquisitely explained Doctorji, "sometimes a point, sometimes a wave." He also taught us an ancient chant and to feel its Sanskrit syllables rolling in our mouth and throat like grapes: *Om namah Shivaya,* or just *Om.*

"It is all you will ever need," he said. "Om contains the vibrations of all consciousness, Om will protect your mind. Om is God Himself."

Eventually, when I was 15, my mother decided the solution to my moodiness was to have me institutionalized, and she found a psychiatrist willing to commit me. There was very little understanding in those days about post-traumatic stress disorder or sexual abuse, both of which I experienced, so I was diagnosed with "schizoaffective disorder." It was a fashionable diagnosis for adolescents at that time, just as it was fashionable to send your "problem child" to a mental hospital.

The doctors at the private hospital in Westchester said I was so ill that I might never function normally, that I would undoubtedly be on heavy medication for years — perhaps even life — and that frequent office visits would be necessary to monitor me.

Desperate, I called Doctorji. He was a psychiatrist, could he not intervene? To his eternal credit, he tried, by meeting with my mother privately. Later, I learned that he offered to work with me himself, offering to see me every day instead of her committing me to the mental hospital. She refused.

The last time I visited him before I was hospitalized, we sat in his little office and he told me to look at his forehead.

"Don't think, don't blink," he said.

He chanted and guided me through a meditation. I imagined he was planting some sort of spiritual-depth charge into my heart, with timers set at intervals for the rest of my life. I was terrified, but, along with the terror, there was a deep sense of peace and confidence; in the timeless place that really mattered, I felt that I was alright and would be forever.

"Go meditate," he said reassuringly, as he closed the door, saying goodbye.

My mother took me away and left me in the Westchester mental hospital for four months where I was subjected to over one hundred shock treatments — electroconvulsive (ECT) and insulin.

I did not see Doctorji for twenty-five years. By the time I did, he'd had a devastating stroke, but he remembered me immediately. Delighted, he turned to his assembled students, "She was with me at the beginning! She was meditating when she was…" He brought his hand low to the floor, to the level of a small child's head.

Later, he explained to me in his idiosyncratic English, "I could do nothing. You were a minor. If you had been a major, I might have done. But your mother…" His words trailed off as he shook his head.

To me, Doctorji was a loving, nurturing, adult friend who I had once needed desperately, and the only person in my world to take a stand against sending a 15 year-old off for ECT. He also gave me, in advance, the antidote that would prevent me from being destroyed by the psychiatrist's treatment: Yoga.

He won my heart with his assurance that, in my true nature, I was inextricably eternal, imperishable, beyond body and mind, of infinite consciousness and infinite joy, and that I would come to realize this by meditating as often as possible. In the hospital, through the terrifying fog of shock treatments, I repeated my mantra as much as I could and I held on for dear life to the assurance that there was something real, something infinitely meaningful beyond what I was experiencing there.

His wisdom is real, I'd tell myself, *and my anxiety is Maya.*

I'd play Doctorji's voice over and over in my head, the slow sonorous roll he'd use to lead guided meditations...*deeply relax your body, feel the flow of electricity from your body to the stars...*I'd read my paperback Gita, which the hospital allowed me to keep, and I'd pretend that I was a yogi preserving equanimity in all circumstances. Eventually, I was released.

I have not often told this story because it's so very painful and personal. But it explains my lifelong devotion to the yoga tradition which saved my life. Without the grounding I received at Ananda Ashram, I am not at all sure I would have survived so many months in an asylum at that age. I have been a mental health counselor myself, as an adult, and the few people I've met who had that many shock treatments back in the 1960s are now permanently under case management. I was very, very fortunate.

Most of us, thankfully, don't have to put our yoga practice to that particular test, though we each have our own life crises and challenges. Our practice can be a real friend and ally.

May we all, in our lifetime, discover this.

I really believe that when we're here right now, when we show up,
that is the gift we can give to the world.
~ Rodney Yee

In Gandhi's Footsteps

Sharon Gannon

In 1982, while living in Seattle, Washington as a dancer, poet, musician and painter, I went to see *The Animals Film,* a British documentary that probed into the relationship between human beings and animals. I went because the sound track was by Robert Wyatt, a musician whom I admired, and because Julie Christie, an Academy Award-winning actress, narrated the film.

Those two hours and twenty minutes in the movie theater altered my life like no other single incident had before. The film exposed the cruel, exploitative, and inhumane way that human beings treat animals, by exploring the use of animals as entertainment (from stuffed toys to pets), as food, as providers of clothing, and as victims of military and "scientific" research. Fortunately, it ended with the Animal Liberation Front (ALF) rescuing the research animals from a laboratory.

The movie caused me to radically rethink art, the purpose of the artist, and what I was doing with my life; if I wasn't contributing to stopping the insanity I saw depicted in this film, what *was* the value in what I was doing?

I had been an on-again, off-again vegetarian before the film but, after viewing it, I became a committed vegetarian and, soon after, a vegan. Deeply affected, I vowed that I would find a way to help stop the suffering of the animals I had seen in the film — but how? When I tried to voice my feelings, my friends accused me of being too emotional, yet I knew that what I had seen was a glimpse into a reality that not many people had or cared to experience, and I could no longer live in such a cushioned state of denial.

I knew that for the situation to change, a whole society had to change — indeed, a whole culture. But first, could there be a change among my friends and myself? Could *I* change? I felt only incredibly inadequate and inarticulate.

While in this state of intense internal turmoil, I fell down some steep, slippery stairs and fractured my fifth lumbar vertebra. The accident resulted in a paralysis of my right leg for a painful and frightening two weeks. I recovered the use of my leg, but would still lose all sensation on occasion when the bone shifted and pinched a nerve. During this time, I moved to New York City. where I began attending yoga classes as a last-ditch effort to do something non-surgical about my pain. Yoga would not only help my back, but would instigate a reintegration of all parts of my being.

During my first few yoga classes, I had a rare and profound experience of going deeply into the feelings of my body as well as into the judgments, assumptions, and opinions of my mind.

Was it painful? Extremely so! But, perhaps for the first time in my very physical life, I was actually being truly physical; I wasn't trying to get *out* of my body — I was actually going deeper *into* it with a sense of adventure.

Previously, I had objectified my body, considering it to be just a tool I needed to exist; after all, I aimed to change the world, save the animals, and bring peace on Earth — and I needed a fit body to accomplish it all!

I came to realize, through my practice of yoga, that ideas alone were not enough to change the world or to change my own life; whatever I wanted to see in the world around me had to first become a reality in my *own* life and in my own *body*, right down to the molecular level. Change had to start with the way I lived, the way I breathed, the way I spoke.

The disease of disconnection that causes us to say one thing while meaning another — and to do a completely different *third* thing — stems from a deep lack of self-confidence. I learned that the unitive power of well-being, which arises through aligning with breath (the animating life force), allows one to feel a part of the community of life rather than feeling at odds with it.

And, through my time on the mat, I also learned about the nature and meaning of karma. I came to realize that how we treat others determines our own reality — we are powerful beings whose actions have an impact. This helped me to see and understand that this impact is not just on the world at large, but on everyone around me and, ultimately, on *myself.* Yoga taught me that life provides us with opportunities to be kind, kindness leads to compassion, and compassion is essential for enlightenment — the goal of yoga.

~ ~ ~

I eventually became an activist — a yoga activist as well as an animal rights activist — someone who actively wants to stimulate change in the world. Pointing fingers and trying to change others is an endless job, and if we can't get to the root of a problem, our efforts only end in frustration.

Yoga offered me an *effective* form of activism because it taught me that there really is no "out there" out there. I realized I create the world I live in. If I want to change what I don't like in the world, I must start by changing what I don't like about myself.

What we see in the world around us is only a reflection of what is inside of us; our present reality is a projection of our inner reality, and that inner reality arises according to our past karmas. Our past karmas are the result of how we have treated others; how we have treated others in the past determines our present reality.

We are in the midst of a global crisis, but many of us don't know what to do about it. The popularity of yoga at this time may be no coincidence. A yogi, by definition, is someone who strives to live harmoniously with the earth and — through that good relationship — strives to purify his or her karma so that enlightenment can arise.

We realize, in the enlightened state of yoga, how important

our relationship to the earth and to other beings really is — how interconnected we are with all of life, how our individual actions matter to the whole.

How we treat others will determine how others treat us, how others treat us will determine how we see ourselves, and how we see ourselves will determine who we are. The cycle to create positive change in the world starts from an enlightened state.

And in my journey, this all starts with yoga.

*Yoga is the technology of love. It is the means to develop
intimacy with Self, with others, and all of life.*
~ *Mark Whitwell*

Bending to Forgive

Linda Handiak

It is said that forgiveness is the ultimate act of love, the ultimate path toward healing, and the ultimate result of opening one's heart. My path toward forgiveness was a long one.

In 1992, I was prescribed a high dosage of antibiotics for a sinus infection. A violent reaction to the medication left my body ulcerated, inside and out. My hair fell out in handfuls, I developed an intolerance to gluten and lactose, and my insides were wracked by spasms that left me flushed, even while I sat quietly at staff meetings. Despite the pain, I never took time off because work and routine were my analgesics; I became accustomed to living just outside of my skin, outside the core of pain, carrying my body with the same detachment I felt toward a bag of items from a garage sale.

My body had failed me, not just as physical machinery but as something that defines a woman. When doctors misdiagnosed me with Crohn's disease and discouraged me from trying to conceive, I stayed late at work to avoid facing the black hole of my social life. I couldn't eat in restaurants, I couldn't go out at night without having to sleep-in the next day, and now I couldn't even have children. *"Who would want me,"* I thought, feeling I was too high maintenance for too little return. I shrank from intimacy, feeling it could only reopen wounds that had begun to scab over with feigned indifference.

I may have functioned as a drone indefinitely had my father's health not also collapsed. He couldn't leave the house for months and my sleep pattern became erratic while I witnessed his doctors unsuccessfully experiment with one treatment after another.

Deciding that I'd be of no use to him if I got sick again, I took up yoga to soothe my insomnia. At first, I was exhilarated by the sense of control it gave me over my weak, unpredictable body; it was very gratifying when my asanas looked right and when I felt my spine lengthen and its knots iron out as I did back bends and seated twists. A faint breeze stirred through forgotten passageways inside me — not dead nor barren, only cluttered and neglected — and cleared space for the real work to begin.

After a few weeks, a very experienced teacher took over the class. The previous teacher usually spoke only when correcting our alignment or breathing; that suited me fine as I equated yogic success with good body form. The *new* teacher was annoying; she pulled the rug out from under me by insisting that we didn't have to *achieve* anything — we didn't even have to try the asanas or push the limits of our bodies if we didn't feel like it. In fact, we didn't have to do *anything*, just *be*.

"What rubbish," I thought. *"Then why even bother coming to class? Maybe yoga has nothing to offer the daughter of hard-working European immigrants."*

My family used to weigh everything we did by its "usefulness." Even as a young teenager, I used to agonize over the usefulness of what I was doing; I felt I had to justify my existence — a memory which catches in my throat. My father had often scorned rest and play, and now his body had turned on him through an autoimmune illness.

In that tenth class, I cried because I couldn't remember the last time I had seen joy in my father's eyes. I cried for the times we shared words but not feelings; in fact, I had spent the last few years protecting myself from feeling too much in general.

Then I realized I was more like my father than I had ever imagined. In high school, both of us had measured our self-worth through grades, and neither one of us could say "no" to colleagues and friends because we cringed from perhaps disappointing them. I couldn't get upset with my father for doing these things because I hadn't worked through them either — I too wanted to be appreciated for what I *did* because I didn't believe that what I *was* may be good enough.

As I touched my forehead to the floor in child's pose, something in me uncoiled, releasing a stream of silent tears. With my eyes averted, I fled the yoga studio but I could no longer flee reality; I couldn't flee my new awareness of myself. It had been a long way down to solid ground.

I continued on my yogic journey and my practice carved

out a vital space during the week for reflection, for prayer and for feeling my emotions without fear — like coaxing a damaged limb back into activity within a protective pool of water. Once the space was cleared, I could add other tools, and re-examined such things as my faith and my relationships. Our yoga teacher taught us that we couldn't give love from a place of self-hatred; my religion exhorted me to forgive others, but yoga taught me to also forgive myself and my body. As I practiced more, I became less frightened of showing my scars, both inside and out.

There is a certain peace that is accessed by going down into the depths and darkness of the soul, like Orpheus, to retrieve something that has been lost. This peace is not the same as the thin calm of the untried soul. When I express to others that we are greater than the sum of our past failures and mistakes, from a place of conviction I can now speak.

And, when my journey takes an unexpected turn, I just breathe into the initial tightening in my chest, into the still-point of confusion, and feel my mind gradually loosen its grip on the outcome it tries to plan. Plans can be reshaped, just as the body can move from one asana to another; change is easier now that I don't pin my self-worth on the success or failure of my work.

Along my path there is still some stiffness of my muscles and my mind and heart, and some days I have doubts; one's limitations don't dissolve overnight, but yoga taught me not to despise them as shortcomings, but rather to respect them as steps along the path of growth.

And steps toward ahimsa for myself.

Reflections

The goal of yoga is peace, not power…
Peace cannot be attained through power,
yet power is the result of peace.
~ T.K.V. Desikachar

Hip Hopping to Yoga

Russell Simmons

I grew up in Hollis, Queens, and, as a young man, I found myself falling into the same traps that ensnare so many other young people growing up on the streets of urban America: I began to get caught up with drugs and gangs. Not because I was a bad person at heart, but because they seemed to be the most powerful ways for me to express myself in that environment.

Like so many others, I would have probably continued making empty investments into that type of expression if I hadn't come into contact with a new force on the streets, a force that was even more powerful than drugs or gangs. That presence was called *hip-hop*.

The very first time I heard hip-hop, I knew my life would never be the same. I knew that I had found a better avenue to express myself and to pursue a better relationship with the world. In hip-hop's powerful beats and rhymes, I heard the truth, and I heard it loudly. I thought this truth prevailed all else.

Then I found the science of yoga.

It was the early 1990s and I was living in Los Angeles, learning my way around the movie business. On the surface, it looked like I had everything: a fancy house, plenty of friends, and was surrounded by beautiful women. But inside, I felt empty. I was financially successful but wasn't at peace. The truth is, I was fearful of real success, fearful of what was around the corner. I wasn't content because I was searching for something real. Thankfully, I didn't have to search for long.

That's because one day, my great friend, Bobby Shriver, dragged me into a yoga class with him. Any doubts I had about doing yoga (my perception being that only gay men practiced it), evaporated pretty quickly once I took a look around. I couldn't believe how many beautiful women were there, bending and stretching and contorting right in front of me! It seemed like every one of them had a better body than the next!

But it was more than the beautiful scenery that excited me. Even though I was struggling with the asanas, I realized that I had stumbled onto something incredible. Just through sweating and focusing on my breath, I began to find more peace than I had ever found in the bottom of a bottle or a line of coke or a Stair Master! When I came out of that class an hour and a half later, I was as high as hell, but it was a beautiful, natural high, without any of the negative baggage that comes with drugs or alcohol. I was hooked. I knew that I had found something special. I had entered a space where there was no fear, no future, no nothing. And I wanted to go back.

I believe that one of the reasons I also had such an instant connection to yoga was my teacher that day, an incredible man named Steve Ross. Steve's very committed to yoga, but he doesn't push it like a religion. He's completely non-judgmental. If he had pushed it hard, I probably would have been turned off the same way I rebelled against organized religion when I was younger. Soon, I was going to yoga every chance I got.

~ ~ ~

Yoga began making me much healthier and happier, but very few of the people around me understood my passion, let alone shared it. They were like, "Man, what are you talking about? What the hell is yoga?" They thought it was something for old white ladies or gay men! And I could understand why. When I went to that first class, there were probably fifty-six women, two gay men, plus me and Bobby, but there was nobody there who looked like me (African-American) or who seemed to come from a similar background. Not because such people were being shut out, but because it simply wasn't on their radar.

The few people who *did* have a vague sense of yoga felt weird about it because they were raised Baptist or Muslim. They didn't understand that yoga really shared the same space as all those other practices — that the messages you find in the yoga scriptures are the same as you'll find in the Bible, the Koran or the Torah. The only difference is that the yogis aren't trying to tell you to separate yourself from other religions. They're letting you know that the sameness is there, that as long as you're getting in touch with God, it's all good. And it was definitely all good for me.

~ ~ ~

I used to disenfranchise myself. I had money, traveled the world, ate in the finest restaurants, stayed in the best hotels and was always surrounded by powerful people. But I struggled with fame and success as much as I had struggled with obscurity and so-called failure. I had money in my pocket, but I *still* worried that I wasn't smart enough.

I still worried that I wasn't talented enough; I still worried that my next idea was going to fail and that people would laugh at me; I still worried that it was all going to end one day and that everyone would say I was just a fluke. And, I still worried that people only wanted to be around me for my money and for what I could *get* them instead of them truly liking and caring about me.

And, to be honest, I *still* ask myself those same questions, though I don't struggle with them as much. They may come into my mind, but through yoga, I am able to push them right out again. Through yoga, I hear God's voice telling me that I am talented and I can hear it reminding me that I am smart and I can hear it telling me that I will realize my dreams with hard work and focus, reminding me that it won't all end tomorrow.

I was reminded of this recently when I was speaking to some students about the power of yoga. After my lecture, one of the students came up to me and said, "Russell, you kept saying how meditation has been one of the keys to your success. But you weren't meditating when Run DMC was big, you weren't meditating when Def Jam first blew up. You got paid all of those times without yoga."

On the surface, he was right. But I also had to tell him he was overlooking a key fact: you see, without the focus and the confidence I gained through yoga, Def Jam would have been the *zenith* of my success. I wasn't the first black guy to make a little money in the record business. My initial success was nothing that Berry Gordy, Quincy Jones or many other talented people hadn't done before me. If I've done something that's fairly unique, I like to think it's being one of the few guys who were able to *build* on their initial success. I like to think that what separates me from the pack is that I didn't piss it all away; I avoided being just another guy who "had it all" then lost it just as quickly.

Yoga empowered me —I married because of yoga; I learned how to drive because of yoga; I became more philanthropic because of yoga; I bought my first house because of yoga; I became more focused because of yoga. Yoga has helped me believe that people love me for who I am instead of who I appear to be.

On so many different levels, my life has more value now because of yoga. I can honestly say that it is the thing that has had the greatest influence on me.

~ ~ ~

So many black and brown people in this country, whether

they've been through addiction or incarceration, have been tragically disenfranchised because of their addictions. I say *tragically* because most people aren't involved with drugs because they're bad people. I believe they're hooked on drugs or alcohol because they have trouble getting the noise out of their heads. And, because they can't afford a doctor and a prescription, they self-medicate. I've been there myself; when I was much younger, I used to get up at dawn and get high because the noise in my head was so loud.

With yoga, I'm not chasing something *de-structive*. I'm chasing the high you get from finally getting your body and mind on the same page. And, that's actually one of the most *con-structive* things you can do.

I think that if everyone consciously started practicing yoga tomorrow, in a year that hood would be a much better place to live. People would be lifting each other up instead of pulling each other down; the streets would be filled with compassion instead of conflict. That's how powerful this yoga thing is.

In fact, I believe that if people who practiced yoga were the only voters in this country, then we really would be the greatest nation on Earth.

Reflections

When the mind and the heart are stretched together in expanding self awareness, there is instantaneous self-transcendence and limitless freedom.
~Sri Swami Nirmalananda

Awareness Beyond Words

Lisa Miriam Cherry

The only thing that we can be truly aware of is that we're aware, I recall my grade four teacher, Mr. Gerwitz, telling our class one day. I do not recall what inspired his profound lesson, but he seemed to be an old soul, ever compassionate and serene, and he struck me as unique.

That day remains crystal clear in my mind. As the entire class seemed to exit in a daze, the girl behind me tapped my shoulder and asked me for the definition of *aware*.

"I think it means *to see*," I hesitantly replied, not even sure how to explain it to myself. With the teacher's words reverberating in my mind, the world seemed to stand perfectly still. Little did I know, I'd been introduced to the concept of *consciousness*: seeing reality for what it truly is, not the realm of illusion perceived by most.

But, in that moment, I was boggled. What did the teacher mean? As I was too shy to ask, his words would linger with me for years in my thirsty quest for answers to the mysticism of the universe: *Is there more to reality than meets the eye? How and why are we a part of it? What is life truly about?* Like the teacher, yoga would serendipitously appear in my life. And the answers to my questions would, as well.

~ ~ ~

It is said that the sun, the moon and the planets explain much about our outlook on life, but I also believe that our rebirth into many lifetimes plays a quintessential role. Perhaps, in this lifetime, my personal path or svadharma was to look "beyond," partaking the role of the Observer, the Witness, the night-time dreamer of prophetic dreams, my soul being ever-curious about the mystery of our existence and how I could learn more about the intricate web of life.

Whenever I'd see Asian actors meditating placidly in their stereotypical movie roles, I felt the answers I sought may lie within; not only did the characters they portrayed seem calm amidst the storms of life, but they seemed to have an understanding, a wisdom, an awareness beyond my own. I aspired to attain such an internal state where I could ride the tides that blew my way. Never did I imagine that I'd one day become a stressed-out journalist and nonprofit director, riddled with severe brain fog from my multiple sensitivities to our daily environment. At the age of 36, I felt like I was losing my mind.

One of my best friends — who had run out of advice for me — told me to try yoga. "I've heard that it changes your perception," Debra said. Well, if it could save my sanity while I was detoxing, so be it, I thought, and by mid-week I was off to a rustic resort north of town. They had yoga classes. The lake was brimming with roaring jetskiiers and screaming children, but I was in heaven — no smog, no cars, and a life about to transform.

Yes, transform. In a turtle-paced class held in a small, musty room reminiscent of a storage space where my fellow yogis were a bedraggled mother and her eight year-old son. The latter, a beacon of inspiration, displayed razor sharp focus and held each asana with bated breath. Admittedly, I did not. *"What's the big deal about this yoga thing?"* my mind kept shouting, feeling as if imprisoned in a slow motion film. By the hour's end, however, a tsunami of energy had rushed through me like a shot of vitamins soaring through my veins.

Driving home to Toronto just afterward, I bee-lined for the nearest yoga studio and ran into their next class. My only regret is that I never thanked the resort's teacher to tell her that she had changed the course of my life.

~ ~ ~

When a traumatic illness strikes and one's entire life is thrown upside down, one may feel as if catapulted from their soul's path. Such was the case as I developed Multiple Chemical Sensitivity, the illness that led me to yoga. My quest for true awareness would be sorely interrupted.

Growing up in a family home regularly doused with toxic cleansers and pesticides and years of exposure to formaldehyde in university anatomy labs had wreaked havoc on my liver and neuroimmune system. Leaky dental fillings containing mercury, lead, and a host of other heavy metals were the straws to break the camel's back.

By my mid '30s, my lead levels were soaring off the doctor's chart and, with symptoms of intense brain fog and spinal tingling from almost every building I entered, I could handle indoor air no longer. Having no "safe home" in either body or mind, I was in fight-or-flight mode in every cell of my body.

With my escalating anxiety went my innate sense of wonder, my eyes which saw beauty in the world, my thrill with the mysticism of it all. I felt like *The Wizard of Oz*'s Dorothy, the Tin Man, and the Scarecrow all in one. I missed my Self and wanted her back. My fear manifested in my not breathing — or my breathing very shallowly — until my low blood oxygen level signaled me to inhale once again. At one point, I even visited a biofeedback clinic to discover why I felt I wasn't breathing.

"You don't stop *breathing*," the flabbergasted clinician sputtered. "You'd be *dead* if you stopped," he added, curtly. "But I'm not breathing!" I protested. He refused to do the test.

Debra's recommendation could not have come soon enough. I don't know whether it was my health or the beginning of my first Saturn Return — an auspicious time, say astrologers, when Saturn's return to the celestial spot it occupied during our precise moment of birth throws us head-first into our next big soul-developing stage of life — which brought me to yoga or yoga to me. But, it was as if a force was drawing me there.

In the first few days, I quickly rediscovered my breath. It returned like a lost child who had finally found her home. My lungs instinctively expanded to fill with deep inhales and smoothly rebounded from deep ujjayi exhales. I emerged from one of my first yoga classes with the thunderbolt-like epiphany that I was finally breathing *normally*, my stomach moving in and out, in and out. I felt like a fish thrown back into the ocean, gratefully in its element once again, oxygen permeating every cell of my being, my rhythms in sync with those of the universe, as if an endless fountain was replenishing my dehydrated soul.

My soul began to yearn for anything yogic, and a quote I read by T.K.V. Desikachar, a revered, Indian teacher who referred to "the ocean of yoga," especially tugged at my core, for I had fallen into this ocean from which I could happily not climb out. When a couple of weeks later I flipped open the Omega Institute's summer calendar and found a workshop entitled *The Ocean of Yoga* that the master himself would be teaching, I knew I was meant to attend. And, to New York's Hudson Valley I ventured.

Desikachar's ocean included all the eight limbs of yoga, with breath, meditation and chanting being equally as important as asanas — as per Patanjali's *Yoga Sutras*, the ancient "bible" on yoga. And, he emphasized individualizing each person's practice, a precept passed down from his legendary father, T. Krishnamacharya. As someone who adheres to holistic philosophy, I knew I was back on my soul's path.

"Yoga is about the mind. Do yoga and you will heal the body, but you will first heal the mind," Desikachar said. Considering my anxiety, the mind was first on my list.

By diving deeply into this ocean and adding to my daily life the powerful practices of meditation and alternate nostril breathing, chanting a powerful Buddhist mantra, *nam myoho renge kyo,* (the title of the Lotus Sutra), and employing a detoxifying mudra whereby my thumb and ring finger connect, I began to feel taller, then felt what I can only describe as a body within my body — an energy or my *soul.* And both my fear and Type A dualistic thinking melted further away.

In their place entered a wisdom which whispered in my ears as I meditated, did my asanas or relaxed in savasana, revealing to me not only my soul's artistic path but also that we are all part of a larger universal web — an insight which let me see love as the force maintaining life on each level, a profound truth of the connection that I could feel at my core.

This connection made itself "visible" to me that summer on Gabriola Island, along the western coast of Canada. There, in a small, sun-filled cedar studio, in the span of one long hour, our class was led through just five asanas and instructed to hold them for an excruciating ten minutes each.

"Focus on your breath," our teacher repeatedly advised.

Upon leaving the studio and re-entering the green wilderness beyond, I viscerally felt this "connection to all" — to the trees, to the sky, to the sparkling, dancing blades of grass. A magnetic connection as if by a web whose strands were connected to my every cell; the soft blades of grass brushing the hairs on my arms; the clouds skimming my scalp; the gentle stare of nearby deer stirring my heart. "Do you feel what I feel?" marvelled a fellow yogini who waded slowly through the grass nearby. I assumed that I did: Heaven on earth. As the great Indian mystic, Kabir, once said, *God is the breath within the breath.*

As my practice developed, I intuitively began to close my eyes and gaze inward toward my heart chakra. Sensations of being filled with a gentle but empowering energy spread across my chest and unfolded down my arms like a warm shielding cloak, opening my heart and gracing my being. I became more open to others, able to experience empathy where I could previously not and able to experience forgiveness for relatives who had judged the validity of my illness for years. Perhaps, I realized, they were just stuck in their vantage point as I once was in mine.

Painful memories appeared to rise and float from my sacrum as I twisted and bent in hip-opening asanas: familiar faces, words, abusive incidents from my past. I was consumed not only by a great safety and inner peace but also by what Patanjali called an unbounded awareness and consciousness — an understanding of not only myself but of those around me and what felt like an understanding of the cosmos at its core. Seeing things for how they really are; seeing reality for what it really is.

Westerners describe this shift from a one-dimensional to a multi-dimensional perspective as a "spiritual transformation," psychologist and author Wayne Dyer describes it as our "getting in the gap," and Carlos Castaneda (a renowned anthropologist and author of such shamanistic books as *The Teachings of Don Juan)* describes it as "a shift of one's assemblage point."

Yoga is said to create a feeling of oneness with the Divine, the quantum field or web which connects us to each other and all, but my practice had provided me with so much more.

~ ~ ~

As young children, we are very aware on some levels, very present in the moment. We know what we like, what sounds like truth, what does not. Our minds are not yet closed by the conditioning of the world. As my practice evolved, I felt a return to the Truth, to my long-lost sense of the mystery of the world, and to my sense of Self within this mystery we call Life.

I was blessed to have a vivid dream one night, featuring an a near-glowing, celestially-radiant being — an angelic woman about seven feet tall, surrounded by a near-blinding white aura from her toes to her thick mane of golden, wavy hair. She glided over to me as I sat meditating in the outer corridor of a grand, Taj Mahal-like building, leaned over, and gently asked that I follow her into a nearby room. Stunned, I hesitated, then rose and followed in anticipation.

Standing in front of me in her long, flowing white gown, she raised her hands to her heart chakra, slowly opening and closing them like flower buds in spring. "Do yoga every day and it will open your heart," she said, her words entering me telepathically. "Do it every day. It will change your life."

And that it was doing. Not only had a greater exuberance burst throughout my heart which had been asleep for years, but I now felt as *one*...with myself, with the breath that blew throughout my being, with the universe that surrounds. I felt like the lotus which rises from the mud to blossom, even amidst the storms of life.

Some say illness is a gift when one opens to the offerings brought along our path. We may find answers our soul has been seeking for lifetimes. Thankfully, I accepted an invitation to try an ancient healing practice and found an answer to my soul's deepest prayers — an understanding of myself, my path, and the universe whose consciousness is connected with our own.

"The only thing that we can be truly aware of is that we're aware," I was taught that fateful day, years ago. It essentially speaks for itself: Our perception of the world around us, if we are not grounded in the present moment, is but an illusion; our awareness — our perception of reality — limited only by our state of mind.

Quiet the mind, put one's self into the immensity of the present moment, and open the floodgates to a vastly truer perception of reality than one might ever imagine — of ourselves, of the world, and of the universe, as well. Having the keys to this mystery was always my deepest desire, and it came to me through the ocean of yoga.

Into an awareness beyond words was I transported. And, with my eight-limbed practice, I can reside in that beautiful world each day.

I look for the energy that flows through all of us and brings
with it a sense of freedom and joy.
~ Angela Farmer

Dancing with the Feminine

Adelheid Ohlig

I came to the study of yoga out of desperation. Desperation, despair and depression. I was in the turmoil of my first year at university, overwhelmed by life, and close to suicide when my brother, a psychologist, recommended that I study yoga. I did, and it returned to me my deep desire to live. Only time would tell whether it could also save me from what was yet to come?.

During my first few years, post-graduation, I had my dream job working long hours as a writer and editor for Reuters and other major news agencies. I was doing well, having a great time, and it seemed like life couldn't get much better. I even started training to be a yoga teacher.

But I would soon be diagnosed with cervical cancer. I couldn't believe it: *Cancer.* My mother died of cancer after numerous operations, radiation treatments and repeated chemotherapy, as did several of my aunts and uncles. Still, I never imagined in my wildest nightmares that this disease would hit *me*. After all, I had what I thought was a healthy lifestyle: eating vegetarian nearly all my life, doing my yoga exercises with regularity since I was twenty, meditating almost every day, and enjoying my work as a journalist.

Cancer? *"No, not me,"* I thought. *"Others, yes, but not me."* And so it happened. I was in my mid-30s and at my gynecologist's for my yearly exam when she told me to come back after three months because there were "very suspicious cells" in my cervix.

I didn't take this seriously. I went to Japan on assignment, traveled throughout Asia, and returned to the doctor a year later. This time, the diagnosis was grim. She told me that the cells in my cervix were malignant and that I had a carcinoma in situ. She then began to explain the normal procedure of operation, radiation and chemotherapy to me and I burst right into tears.

I did not want that, I told her. "Are there any other options?" Her answer was an emphatic "NO." I left the office, crying.

The next few weeks were spent visiting other doctors, having PAP smears taken, and hearing the same cervical cancer diagnosis. I thought of my relatives and how they had died horrifically despite following doctors' orders to operate, radiate and opiate. I then watched my cat and other animals. What did they do when they were sick? Certainly not go to a hospital. Well, nor would I.

I searched for alternatives and found a general practitioner who was supportive of my ideas on self-healing and who promised to help me with prescriptions although this wasn't the normal medical approach. Now I had an ally and I began to have hope. I also found women who'd had the same Class 5 PAP diagnosis as me and who had chosen routes other than surgery —and found that alternatives had worked for them.

I probed deeper. I began to reflect and seriously take stock of my lifestyle and realized that the idea of working long hours at my high-tech job just didn't seem right. Not only was my entire life organized around my job, but I became aware that I did my exercises not out of *joy* but rather from a sense of *duty*.

I meditated and listened and waited. Then I heard it: a small, quiet voice. It came from the depth of my being, telling me that although what I was doing in the world was valuable and rewarding, it was no longer really satisfying my inner longings. Work was easy, colleagues were friendly, my travels were exciting and stimulating, but I was not *content*. And, truth be told, I was bored not only with my job, but also with yoga and my life. The question now was: *What do I want to do? What would bring me happiness and joy?*

Living involves choosing. And the choice is ultimately about *cutting* — something will have to be cut and you get to decide. Do you choose the cut in your body (via an operation) or in your life by letting go and making changes?

Empowered by this realization, I chose to "cut out" my job. Then I chose to take time out for myself. I received acupuncture, took homeopathic remedies and got massages regularly. I also injected myself with mistletoe extract, went into psychotherapy, and took lessons in breathing and a form of musical healing called *sounding*. I tried diets and oil massages, got in touch with my feelings, and went through rage, disillusionment, grief and numbness. Yet, while such therapies alone may have brought about the healing of others and did help me feel somewhat better, they weren't my final answer.

I then wondered, *"Could connecting with my feminine self and getting my cycles back bring about a change in consciousness, a change in lifestyle that would support and promote a healthy female body?"* Perhaps I needed to get in touch with my fears about being a woman and what that meant?

As I journeyed deep into my fears, what came up for me was anger at the invalidation of the feminine by the patriarchal structure we all live in: If you are a woman, then you are not important. Look at the way our cycles are treated — in our society, menstruation should be hidden and sanitized, childbirth should be in hospitals and sanitized, and menopause should not be experienced at all. No honoring or importance. Apparently, women should be forever young. It's no wonder that as I rose to the top of my profession in a male-dominated field, I stopped cycling. I had, in effect, become "the best man for the job."

Still exploring my cycles as a possible answer, I learned about a dancer, physical therapist and yoga teacher in Israel, Aviva Steiner, who had discovered a series of exercises that could induce menstruation and ovulation, even in post-menopausal women. I went to meet Aviva and, after studying with her for only a couple of days, I started menstruating for the first time in three years. I felt elated — elated because I had regained my menstruation which meant I was regaining my health.

These exercises were exactly what I had been looking

for, not only for my health but also for my career. There was something here that I could explore, something that excited me, something that challenged me. Life was fun again — full of joy, full of happiness, full of hope. I stayed with Aviva, studied with her for several months, and learned how to breathe into my sexual organs. I learned how to move my pelvis slowly, sensually, and vigorously. I learned to let myself be, to let myself feel.

I then experimented with her dances and added in yoga asanas that gave me joy because I dared to adapt them to my body — a woman's body. This was the birth of *Luna Yoga*. It was also the grand disappearance of my carcinoma in situ. (I went and got tested again!).

The result: a Class 1 PAP test; a diagnosis of healthy cells. Since I couldn't believe it, I had the cells of my cervix tested a total of *three times*, at three different institutes. The verdict: unanimously Class 1.

I had done it. For two years, I had trusted my own inner wisdom as it led me to leave my job, experiment with alternative therapies, confront my fears, and learn to honor my feminine self. In the process, I had healed and "wholed" myself. And, I had created a form of bodywork that was based on yoga, integrated other body therapies, and respected differences between us all.

I felt powerful and vibrantly alive. And, twenty-five years later, I still do.

The essence of devotion is the yearning of the soul
to return unto itself.
~ Ram Dass

Mother Teresa, my Yoga
Master, and my Self

Father Joe Pereira

It is rare to have a life so blessed that not only one yogic sage but two enter and change the course of your life, but I have been well-blessed.

I was born in a remote village about sixty kilometers away from the city of Bombay and come from a Catholic family with a Portuguese background. Ours is a 400 year-old Christian lineage of a Portuguese colony in India, so we have a blend of an Indo-Portuguese culture.

As a young boy in school, my first encounter with yoga was with a Master who usually taught us traditional subjects like math and science but, one day, demonstrated to me a couple of yoga asanas, one of which is known as the "mandala." In it, you go on your head, and instead of lifting your legs up, you move your legs right around your body. I was fascinated, but it would be several years before I'd encounter yoga again.

When I finished school, I joined the diocese seminary for ten years of an almost monastic life — a very heavy discipline of spirituality. Ironically, I came out of these ten years very intellectually but not spiritually prepared, as there was no reference in our spiritual teachings related to the body.

And the body, I would soon discover, is one of the keys in reaching God.

It was 1968, and I was a newly-ordained priest in Bombay, attending a concert by a renowned violinist, Yehudi Menuhin. At the end of the concert, he brought B.K.S Iyengar up on stage and said jokingly, "This is my new violin instructor," and I recognized Guruji immediately from a yoga demonstration he'd given at the university.

Afterward, I walked up to him and asked, "Do you have classes in Bombay?" He replied, "Yes, I have classes in Bombay, but I am having a problem because the classes are in a school run by a church and they are not quite happy about yoga."

Apparently, the church didn't want to renew his contract, but, when they saw that he was teaching not only me but also another Jesuit man, and realized that I was a priest, they gladly let him continue. It would mark the lovely beginning of my more than forty years as a regular student of Guruji.

Back then, I used to do a lot of singing and was known as "The Singing Priest" in Bombay. I appeared healthy, but was really facing dire health issues. I rarely exercised except to sometimes play cricket, so I would occasionally have severe bouts of throat infections and colds.

But Guruji made a tremendous contribution to my health — and I would need *great* energy down the line to help the marginalized, such as the addicted and HIV Aids patients, through yoga.

For example, I come from a family that has hereditary hypertension. I looked at my blood pressure one day and suddenly noticed that it was 140/90 — not good for a yogi. I rushed to Guruji and he helped me so beautifully that today, at the age of 66, I have a blood pressure of 115/75, which is superb. This baffles "medical people."

They ask, "How do you do this without taking any medication?"

"Only with yoga," I say.

God first sent Guruji on my path, then sent Mother Teresa who I encountered in 1971 when I visited her home, Ashadaan (defined as Gift of Hope), as a new priest in Bombay. We met during a crucial time in my life, as a lot of my companions in the priesthood had quit and gotten married and I, too, was in a crisis of authority. But Mother asked me not to leave.

"Don't quit, stay on, hang on. Jesus needs you," she pleaded.

When I initially met Mother, she said it may take ten years for me to realize my purpose. And she was right. Exactly ten years later, in 1981, while working in Bombay, I helped three of her patients recover from drug addiction and alcoholism with a yoga program I'd devised. Mother was so touched that she called me to also do this work in Calcutta.

There, I started working not only with her other patients, but also with her Missionaries of Charity nuns, preaching at their annual retreats and offering mass in their homes all over India.

When Mother came to know that I was teaching yoga to the nuns, she asked me, "What is this?" And I said, "You know, Mother, your nuns get up early in the morning at 4:30. They all sit very obediently in the chapel at 5:00 to meditate, and half the number of heads are dozing off. Yoga will bring them to be fully present."

She said, "Okay, but you know I have a doctor, Sister Shanti. She's a member in our council and it would be nice for her if you could talk to her about it." I replied, "Definitely."

Fortunately, Sister Shanti welcomed the idea of my teaching yoga to the nuns. Even Mother tried yoga — japa yoga — when a renowned Benedictine monk, Laurence Freeman, introduced her to repeating the phrase *"maranatha,"* meaning *"come Lord,"* as a centering, meditative chant, durng a week-long meditation retreat.

With Mother's blessing, I'd preach to her nuns in Calcutta in the mornings, and in the evenings I'd teach them Iyengar yoga and pranayama. After that, Mother would sit with me and see that I had dinner right away, always insisting that I have an extra chapatti — Indian bread!

But my destiny — to work with the addicted in India on a large scale — took hold when I formally started the program that would become The Kripa Foundation, to aid drug addicts, alcoholics and those with HIV. With Mother's help, I teamed up with all of her homes, helping these poor souls who had also become in-patients. Eventually, she inaugurated our first facility in Calcutta and many more in the years to follow. Because of Mother, I was able to bring yoga to thousands of destitute on India's streets and in her homes. She helped me to find my soul's path, which unfolded beautifully.

At one point, during one of the biggest riots in Bombay as we were driving to safety, Mother turned to me and said, "You must go to our priests' centre in New York and join them."

Her assistant, Sister Audrey, pleaded, "Mother, Father Joe is already doing good work and he's doing the work that you inspired him to do. Don't grab him!" Mother had a good laugh. Now, whenever I preach at a retreat to Mother Teresa's nuns, they introduce me with only one sentence: "This is the priest whom Mother loved."

~ ~ ~

One could call Mother, who was a brilliant person, a *jnana yogini* (yogi of knowledge). But she was also a *bhakti yogini* (yogi of devotion) and she was a *karma yogini* (yogi of service). As was Guruji.

In Guruji's case, he taught me about three sections of yoga which helped both myself and ultimately those I would teach: the outer body pursuit and the inner body pursuit which consists mainly of breathing and withdrawal from the preoccupation of the senses, and the third dimension known as the *spiritual dimension*. This all-important latter dimension, I would say, is a state of experiencing the transcendent: True self-acceptance, not self-denial.

Most of us in the Roman Catholic Church have sacrificed having a life that includes marriage and, with spirituality in the seminaries not addressing our sexuality, this sacrifice is not good. It's a suppression which eventually bursts in one's face, as many men of the church have experienced, ruining the lives of hundreds of child abuse victims and their perpetrators, as well.

With yoga, however, I am blessed that I do not have to deny the fact that I am a sexual human who is beautiful before God. I have learned not only self-love but also heart-opening yogic sequences which develop the beauty of being both a sexual celibate and a sexual human being, and these sequences fulfill me. Yoga's methodology, being one of self-acceptance, lets me truly celebrate my life.

All the mystics over millenia have spoken about the prayer of the heart — which yoga is completely. Because of Guruji, yoga became for me a way of life and I developed a passion for it that has a double dimension: personal growth plus personal and community empowerment. Through the science of yoga, I developed a deep recognition of the supreme yogi, Jesus, the Word of God, because He said, "The Father and I are one," and prayed that we may become one. Yoga is all about feeling that.

For me, Jesus was an Easterner, not a Westerner, as He spoke very yogic statements such as: *If you want to really gain your life, you have to be ready to lose it; Lose yourself in Me; A grain of wheat, unless it falls onto the ground and dies, bears no fruit.*

These are all rich yogic teachings and He definitely would have had to be in a state of yogic disposition to be able to spend those long hours in prayer.

Jesus is my ultimate role model and my "sushumna," with Mother and Guruji being the ida and pingala, respectively, of my spiritual teachings. Like the ida and pingala, subtle body channels carrying powerful currents of spiritual ascetism, they both helped create the flow of compassion along my bodily sushumna, my governing channel.

I have found, over the course of my life, that God never gives us remarkable encounters with sages such as Mother Teresa and Guruji Iyengar just for our own sake, and I repaid this blessing, in 1981, by founding The Kripa Foundation. Eventually we created fifty-one facilities across India. All by the grace of Mother Teresa and Guruji, true yogis at the core.

Today, my yoga practice is absolutely as regular as my Mass, my Eucharist; my celebration of the Mass and my practice of yoga are parallel. Yoga became my way of life and will be to the end of my days.

There is only one religion, the religion of love.
There is only one language, the language of the heart.
~ Swami Sivananda

My Yogic Tree of Life

Rabbi Joseph Gelberman

I have been a yogi for over fifty years and a Kabbalist for over seventy-five years. I was the first rabbi to study yoga and I decided to combine the two into a morning meditation to keep me happy and alive. It all started when I met some of India's most renowned yogis in New York. How did they inspire an hassidic Hungarian rabbi to take up yoga? Let me tell you...

All the swamis who left India to bring yoga to America somehow found me — or I found them! We became friends and I became interested in what made them yogis.

Initially, I met Swami Vishnudevananda, the first yogi to settle down here in New York. We met almost forty years ago and I loved him immediately. His office was on the fourth floor and my synagogue was on the first, and we usually finished work around the same time.

I was heavy-set, so he told me, "You should take up yoga. I'll teach you myself — not in the class, just you and I."

So we turned my apartment into a yoga studio.

I became good friends with Swami Devananda. Once a week, he'd come over and insist, "Let's do it!" It was very difficult for me as I was heavy and couldn't do all the exercises, especially the headstands. But we did it, we laughed a lot, and one day he declared, "I'll appoint you as a professor of yoga!"

"But what am I going to teach?" I asked him. "You're going to teach how *not* to do yoga!" he teased. That was Vishnu's humor for you!

Next, I met Swami Satchidananda, the founder of Integral Yoga. We were invited to speak in a church, he as a swami and I as a rabbi. When I left my rabbinical robe in the church hall and went to the bathroom, I came back to find that he was wearing my robe.

I looked at him and asked, "What is the meaning of this?"

He said, "Don't you know? In a previous life, *I* was the rabbi and *you* were the swami!" So that was a good beginning; in other words, I meet this swami for the very first time, and he has a sense of humor and has something profound to say! And we became very, very good friends. We met very often and he came to my Hebrew classes that I used to teach. Eventually, I thought that maybe he was right — that I was a Hindu in a past life! I love Chinese food — maybe I was once Chinese too!

For some reason, most of the people who were interested in Hinduism and yoga back then were young Jewish men and women, and their Jewish parents were frantic and came for my advice. I didn't know much about yoga except that I had met these swamis.

My first answer to the parents was, "There is nothing to worry about. Let's find out what they teach. Your own rabbi is doing this, so it must be kosher!"

Embracing yoga was easy for me because my kabbalistic teaching was "to be at one with all people." I was teaching this in Judaism. I believe that whether a prayer is said in Hindi or Hebrew or Latin it makes no difference, as long as these are involved: body, mind, heart and soul.

Yoga felt wonderful. Before, I didn't pay any attention to my body, but the body is very important. So I tried to do my best, and eventually I developed a new kind of exercise: *Kabbalah in Motion*. It consists of simple movements, yogic breathing and kabbalistic mantras. At 98 years young, I still do it today. People love it. I wouldn't even call it a religion, but a *philosophy*.

We are not only a body — we also have a mind, heart and soul. This realization is important and is very often missing in some peoples' yoga. When I do my yoga, I feel energized because my body, mind, heart and soul are all together.

~ ~ ~

Integrating Judaism is very important to me. Meditation puts us in touch with God, and *Kabbalah in Motion* is a moving-meditation. Even those who have never studied the Bible or the Torah or Talmud can benefit. It begins with the sure knowledge that all people are *one*, and ends with the *feeling* of this.

There is a famous prayer, "Listen O Israel — everybody listen." What is the message? That there is only one God. So that means there is only one family of mankind. The idea that *"we're white"* or *"we're black"* — that's all stupid! It doesn't fit. We are all children of the one God, and that means we are all brothers and sisters.

In my synagogue, I have a phrase, a teaching for everyone: *There is only one God*, or *Sh'ma Yis'ra'eil, Adonai Eloheinu, Adonai Echad*, in Hebrew. So instead of killing each other, as we do now, we should embrace and love each other. During the Second World War, America could have saved at least half of the six million Jews who were slaughtered. But they didn't listen to their hearts.

When I found yoga, I was still reeling from the deaths of my five year-old daughter, my first wife, my parents and twelve of my seventeen siblings in the concentration camps of the Holocaust. The heart of my life had been ripped away. My grief for the loss of my beloved will never cease, but yoga and Kabbalism opened my heart to the beauty of life once again.

~ ~ ~

People don't realize that we were created for a purpose. The purpose is to for everybody to help God make the world a better place. He can't do it by himself. The kabbalistic interpretation of life makes everything more meaningful, more purposeful. Today, God would say, "I give you an eleventh commandment: Thou shalt have purpose."

We are God's partners. God needs people here in the world. Angels he needs in heaven, but he needs every human being to be an angel here on earth. Satchidananda was one of my angels. He was teaching yoga and I was teaching Judaism (and eventually my kabbalistic version of yoga), and it was a very important part of my life that we did this together. I miss him a lot, and I talk to his spirit every day.

~ ~ ~

Judaism is called the *Etz Hayyim* or *The Tree of Life*. The Orthodox picture this tree with a circle around it, suggesting only *this* is Judaism; that is, only the Orthodox way is Judaism. I never left the circle, although the circle was uncomfortable for me. Instead, I began to explore my roots, expanding the circle. I asked, *"Who am I? How much of the Jewish tradition can I keep and still be a modern man living in this century?"*

There are similarities in the old movement of Hassidism, and within the Jewish religion of today. They emphasize worship through joy, the *simcha* concept; worship through service, the *avodah* concept; and worship through purpose, the *kavanah* concept. These relate to the faith and discipline that Swamiji described so eloquently.

When he described the quest for happiness, meditation and service, he related it to the psychological, existential formula for living and growing, asking "who am I" and "what am I feeling?" These questions refer to our social obligation to our fellow man and society, and to our dedication to God — and our cosmic role in perfecting creation as a partner to God.

In the Kabbalah, when you come to a word and you like

the word, it's meaningful, but to actually know the kabbalistic meaning of that word, one needs to separate it into its letters. If you take the word *yoga* and look at it kabbalistically, you would say that the *"Y"* means to say *yes* to everything, to really enjoy life, to experience everything, and that *"O"* represents always being *optimistic*. Everybody's concerned about the economy but there have been bad times before, so *"G"* represents a *belief in God*; God loves us. And *"A"* would represent *awareness*.

In the very beginning, I was frightened of yoga, but I came to the conclusion that it could help me; it's not about giving up a philosophy, but *adding* something instead. That's what I teach. For example, if to be a real yogi, I have to give up my Judaism, that's not right. If it's not "instead of," that makes more sense.

God gave a part of his wisdom to each of the religions. We all have a part of God in each of us, and we must come together to understand his wisdom completely. As I said earlier, whether a prayer is said in Hindi, Hebrew or Latin makes no difference, as long as these are involved: Body, mind, heart and soul.

Over time, by adding yoga to my life, I was able to hear the still, small voice of my divine soul.

You will too. Just listen to your heart.

Reflections

The Earth to us is an intelligent, living being.
It is able to talk to us and guide us in what to do if we pray
and open up to it, and come into harmony with it.
~ Sun Bear (Native American Bear Tribe Elder)

In My Wildest Dreams

Danny Paradise

Thousands of years ago, as the ancient rishis sat on the banks of the Indus River, meditating or doing asanas, they weren't doing so to lose weight, to get in shape for running or to become more flexible. They were zoning out, entering a deep quiet, connecting with themselves and connecting with the oneness or energy that many call God or the Great Spirit.

They would have looked at me in great amusement, as I didn't have a clue as to what this Great Spirit could possibly or even remotely be. But it would be my wildest dream to find out.

I slid into this dream by studying the martial arts of karate, kung fu and tai chi in my early teens, thanks to my older brother, Mike, my first spiritual guide in life. He introduced me to Masumi Tsuroka, a great force of energy and the father of karate in Canada. Unbeknownst to me, his teachings would help me move easily into the practices of hatha yoga, years down the road. Years, songs, and many adventures down the road...

The road began when Mike moved to the island of Oahu in the Hawaiian chain in the '60s with his wonderful wife, Sharon. When I first visited them in 1968, I was completely overwhelmed by the island's natural beauty. It was then that I realized what I wanted and needed to do before making any career decisions: an exploration around the world. Playing the guitar was my first love but, I wondered, could there be more? I worked the following year at university, saved money and planned my big adventure. At 19 years young, I was off to explore Europe.

Initially I chose to hitchhike for several months throughout England, France, Belgium, Holland, Switzerland, Italy and Spain, then I opted for a world completely foreign to me: southeast Asia and Thailand. This gentle Buddhist nation was overwhelming as the people were the kindest and most hospitable that I had ever encountered, taking the words generosity and happiness to new levels of meaning.

Once, when I ended up at a huge party on the Burmese border in a remote village of northern Thailand, a whole village came by the Thai house where I was entertaining the locals with my guitar, pulled out their Beatles' song books and sang along in the only English they knew. In a country without TV and long before the internet, the powerful band's message of love and peace was well understood even in the midst of the raging Vietnam War next door.

A short while later, on the streets of Taipei, I spotted an absolutely radiant character with a huge round pack on his back, a guitar swinging from the end, and batik paintings overflowing from his bag. Then, on a cargo ship traveling from northern Taiwan to southern Japan, I saw this wild man again! When our ship stopped for the afternoon on an island in the remote edge of the Okinawan chain, I immediately struck up a conversation with him. His name was Arie and he'd been traveling non-stop for eight years.

After being stationed with the Dutch army in Egypt, he traveled down the Nile to its source at Victoria Falls, and made his way to South Africa where he rode with a "cattle drive" across the Kalahari desert.

He told me that his biggest dream was to go to the Amazon, build his own boat, and travel every tributary possible. When I met him, he was just 29 years old and he had traveled (mostly walked) through ninety-eight countries with no sign of slowing down. His living dream of travel influenced me my entire life. I wondered, would I end up in some suburb in Canada in a 9-to-5 job or would I continue to travel and explore this magical world as he did?

Dreaming of returning to Hawaii, I flew to Oahu in 1973, and met up with a surfer friend who got me auditions to sing and play guitar at Waikiki nightclubs. This led to gigs for two years, then I heard about Lahaina's new Blue Max Club, an exotic open-air venue overlooking the ocean, and to Maui I flew. Young people were coming there from all over North America, many of them to escape the industrialized cities, the pollution, cars, noise, and bad news from Vietnam. For housing, I'd sleep on the beach; for money, I played at the Blue Max.

One day, my girlfriend, Jeannie Miller (who had turned to yoga and a vegetarian diet, eventually overcoming cancer of the uterus), introduced me to an amazing man she was studying yoga with: Cliff Barber. He was vibrant, intelligent and 44 years old, had taken vows of renunciation and was living in a cave in one of the giant Hawaiian valleys. Tall, strong and healthy, he had long, darkish blond hair, a long beard, excellent posture, and didn't wear shoes. As I got to know him, I discovered he had studied scriptures of all spiritual traditions and that he had a vast understanding of many different philosophies and mystical traditions including yoga. *And* that he had practiced yoga for nine years just from reading *Integral Hatha Yoga* by Swami Satchidananda.

So, when Cliff was told by two young yoga teachers, David Williams and Nancy Gilgoff, the first western adepts of Pattabhi Jois of India, that they would soon teach the most advanced forms of Ashtanga yoga on Maui (following their premier teaching in Encinitas, California), he informed all of his friends. And, on May 1st, 1976, my one-year anniversary on Maui, a large group of us were privy to a mind-blowing demonstration.

The next morning, everyone who had attended was invited to learn the primary series of Ashtanga yoga at the historical site of the Seaman's Prison garden and, over the next several months, at stunning parks along Lahaina's coast. I recalled the same joyful feeling of energy coursing through my body that I'd experienced during my marital arts days with Master Tsuroka, and welcomed learning this gentler practice of yogic energy movement with open arms. My yogic journey had begun.

~ ~ ~

Before I began yoga, at 23, I had stopped being disciplined physically. I had music as my art, but anxiety and worry had overtaken my psyche. My purpose was undefined and the concept of evolution — which became more important to me as time went on — was beyond my comprehension.

In my first session with David and Nancy, during my first sun salutation's Downward Dog, I broke into a deep sweat and felt my muscles, tendons and my nervous system in a way that I had never experienced before. As my daily practice continued and I moved deeper into the sequences, I also noticed that I felt more in the present moment and my life force seemed to expand. Some days, especially when learning a new sequence of asanas, I went through great toxic eliminations, developing flu-like symptoms soon after.

Each physical shift was accompanied by deeper revelations and awareness. As I came to stillness each day through these meditative practices, I gained new clarity, realizing that there was nothing to worry about, nothing to fear. Yoga, with its powerful emphasis on breath and purification, brought me back each day to a sense of well-being and to a profound feeling of wholeness and joy — even when the physical changes became almost more than I could bear.

One of these changes happened while I was learning the advanced (third) series of Ashtanga yoga, in my third year of practice. I awoke one morning with tremendous chest pains and   could barely breathe. I wasn't sure what was going on. I asked everyone, including a doctor. As David and Nancy were in India, I finally found Cliff and told him my symptoms. He nonchalantly answered, "Oh that's the *saraswati nadi* ... it covers the entire chest and solar plexus. Saraswati is also the goddess of the first musical instrument." Cliff explained that because of the depth of the third series practice, my bone structure was opening and changing.

Bad postural habits that had fixed my bones into unnatural positions were being changed daily by the deep symmetry of yoga practice. When I played music in a club that night, I had no pain, but each time I took a break, I felt almost crippled. The next day, I broke into a deep fever and sweat, and wandered off into the forest where I had an experience beyond my wildest dreams; I felt connected to nature on a dimensional level so deeply beyond words, that deva spirits seemed to be in communication with me.

As the fever subsided and my hallucinations modified, all of my pain disappeared and I recognized a tremendous shift in my awareness and sensitivity. My body was healed and my new posture dawned. I had experienced a deeper communication with nature than ever before and realized that we can communicate directly to the Great Spirit at any time and receive clear messages back. As I'd soon learn, more wild things were in store for me.

Yoga was a powerful physical discipline, but its principle was about relaxing completely, and this became a guiding force in my life. In my meditations, I gained insight that these practices had been passed on to humanity from nature for the purpose of helping people create their lives with wisdom and artistry.

When I began teaching yoga internationally in Goa, India, in 1982, with Cliff Barber, I had a powerful near-death experience that helped me understand that yoga was also a tool of survival. I was stung by a jelly fish in remote waters of the Arabian Sea, yet managed to make it to shore where I collapsed with tremendous pain throughout my body and went into anaphylactic shock; my lungs stopped functioning and within a couple of minutes, I realized that I might not survive. I couldn't speak, move or breathe, and no one else was on the beach.

Over the next four hours, I *forced* myself to breathe, bringing oxygen deep into my lungs every minute or two. Because I had been practicing yoga and pranayama daily for almost eight years, I had developed the strength to control my inhalations even though my normal breathing processes had shut down. In a deeply altered, near-death state and in communication with my soul, I felt like I was being crucified on the beach. An Indian fruit seller that I knew passed by and looked at me but I could not move or say a word. Later, I discovered she had found my friends and told them that she had seen me on the beach and that I was dead!

After more than four hours of my gasping for breath whenever I could, someone sat down beside me. I whispered that I was in shock and needed help. Thankfully, they rushed me to a hospital and the antihistamine injection I received regulated my system back to normal.

But it was my *yoga practice* that had ultimately allowed me to survive, for, during the hours that I struggled to stay alive, I was in what can only be described as clear communication with the heart of the universe. Her message was clear: the practices of yoga were saving my life.

I now saw that not only was I creating my own evolutionary process and my own reality, but that I could also take responsibility for my own physical, psychological and spiritual healing through the work I was doing on myself. My life expanded, my life force increased, and I was instilled with a renewed sense of joy. Communication with the Great Spirit became my way of life.

~ ~ ~

The revelations I experienced in the forest during my healing process taught me of the deeper dimensions of existence and the reality of nature spirits who guide and communicate with mankind. I came to understand that yoga is "soul work" and that our mind and body are tools for the creation of our soul's desires; we each create our own journey and all the challenges that come along with it. God as nature and God as love became realities to me as never before, and I now felt that passing along the teachings I had learned was to be my life's work. But only by invitation, a guiding principle I learned from Cliff.

Each group I worked with became sacred to me, and I determined to be as strong and clear as my teachers — mentally, emotionally and spiritually — to be able to pass on the healing force of yoga to all I met. The miracle of existence, the blessing of having a human body, the awareness of the powerful presence of the Great Spirit and its boundless intelligence and love became guiding principles in my life.

After ten years of teaching in countries around the world, the supreme guitarist, Dominic Miller, introduced me to Sting resulting in my being invited to teach the primary series of Ashtanga yoga to the great singer and his wife, Trudi. Invitations from Paul Simon, Madonna and many other celebrities followed, and I soon realized another of my life's responsibilities: to pass on the ancient yogic teachings to these people as clearly, safely and compassionately as I possibly could, not only for their own personal healing but because of the influence they potentially had.

This year, I celebrate thirty-five years of practicing Ashtanga yoga, a practice which affirms in me a magical sense of reality each day — about the nature of life on Earth, about my own evolutionary journey, and about the beautiful, endless magnificence of the Great Spirit that guides my way.

Health is wealth, peace of mind is happiness.
Yoga shows the way.
~ Swami Vishnu-Devananda

The Ocean of Healing

Katherine Culp

Four decades ago, in the newly-pharmaceutical '60s, before alternative medicine and yoga were accepted into our global consciousness, I was diagnosed with severe rheumatoid arthritis.

The disease affected all of my bones, even my rib cage, the prognosis being that I would eventually end up living in a wheelchair. I was just 15 years old and mortified to have what I considered "an old person's disease." The pain crawled through the muscles and joints of my hands, knees and feet such that it hurt me to move at all — like when one wears a shoe size too small and can hardly walk by the day's end.

The doctors bandaged part of my illness with a drug company's delight: a daily regimen of several cortisone tablets and aspirins which kept my fingers and toes from becoming severely swollen. But the regime wasn't completely without its repercussions. My hair became almost like straw — very brittle and dry — and the twelve aspirins, which I took each day, caused immense water retention and bloating of my thin face and body. I'd bruise if merely *touched*, so my arms and legs appeared fairly black and blue. A crippling rigidity developed in my body overnight should I miss my hourly drugs. With them, I was sore but not swollen and crippled, so I usually just accepted the pain.

I thought the disease would continue forever, and ordered my family to never discuss it in my presence. As for my friends, they never found out my truth — I just told them I was tired or anemic, an excuse which may have been my first step toward healing because, when one dwells on a problem, it sometimes just grows.

To further confuse them, I'd do everything they'd do — staying up late and more. I'd simply rest longer the next day! Wanting to be "normal," I just carried on. But inside, I was very angry, especially because I had won a scholarship to the Royal Academy of Ballet when I was 13. Realizing I'd no longer become the next prima ballerina, all I could do was cry.

After about two years of feeling sorry for myself, I decided to ask God to show me what to do next. One of the answers came in a book my father brought home for me. It was about Edgar Cayce, known as the "sleeping psychic." My father wasn't too impressed with the book, but I read it with a passion and began following some of the treatments that Cayce prescribed: honey and apple cider vinegar drinks, juice fasts, castor oil packs and eating apples galore. I also took sunbaths all for the positive effects of UV light. All of this helped to some degree, giving me great hope and a feeling of not being so alone.

Around this time of exploration, I began researching others involved in alternative health, one being the late Paramahansa Yogananda, author of *The Autobiography of a Yogi*. I read this book reverently and it became like a bible for me, helping to shift my attitude about disease and, of course, compelling me to try yoga.

My doctor didn't want me to exercise much but, being young, I ignored him and checked out the YMCA downtown. It was the 1960s and yoga wasn't yet hip, but I found a class that had about six other girls my age. As no special yoga attire existed in those days, I just dawned my old ballet leotard and tights.

The first thing that impressed me was the yoga teacher. I was accustomed to ballet teachers being flexible, slim and beautiful, even in their forties, but never before had I witnessed a slim, graceful, gray-haired woman who could put her foot behind her head — *and* remain calm!

She was about 70 years old and would repeatedly chastise us for being young girls of 18 and 19 who couldn't even touch our toes; *she* could do it, she said, so why couldn't we? Rather than sounding like criticism, it sounded like a challenge; nonetheless, I never told her that I had arthritis — I just let her think that I was too lazy and out of shape, too ashamed to tell her more.

She taught us the Sivananda method of yoga which entails practicing just a few postures, holding each as long as once can bear it, then releasing the asana for a few minutes before going on to the next. I built up to holding each for three minutes, then I'd relax deeply afterward. This gave me the opportunity to really *feel* my painful body, then to feel a great release when I'd surrender in corpse pose at the end of class. And what a powerful surrender it was; over time, I actually began to appreciate, equally, both the pain of the postures and the pleasure of our ten minute savasana.

After the course ended, I practiced on my own for about one hour each morning and evening, using not only the postures that I'd learned but also the guidance from Swami Satchidananda's renowned book, *Integral Yoga Hatha.*

Opening and closing my practice with the sound *Om,* and always thanking my illness for the teachings I received, I'd send my painful body *love* and thank the arthritis for teaching me what I needed to learn most — *both* patience and love. You could even say that best friends we became.

In 1972, two years after I began practicing yoga, I traveled to Jamaica for a few months to contemplate my life. There, sitting on the beach in Negril, in a state of unbridled tranquility, gazing at the endless blue, watery horizon, I made a brave decision: I'd stop taking the cortisone and aspirins and, if I started to swell, I would just resume taking them once again. Much to my amazement, I didn't swell up over the next few days and realized that my rheumatoid arthritis was no more.

When I returned home to Montreal, I considered verifying my self-prognosis with my doctor, but decided against it — he'd probably just say that it was one of those rare cases where illnesses vanish. *"What's the point,"* I asked myself, as I felt fine.

Years later, however, out of sheer curiosity, I relented, and visited another doctor for a checkup. As I thought would happen, my test results painted a picture of perfect health. And, the doctor questioned what I presumed he would — whether I actually ever *had* the arthritis.

"If so," he smugly exclaimed, "you'd be in a wheelchair by now."

Did yoga cure me? Well, not only did my arthritis disappear, but I witnessed my thoughts shift from ones of anger to ones of love, from non-acceptance to acceptance. This changed everything. When I began to ask, "What is my illness is trying to teach me?" the arthritis no longer appeared totally negative, and I began to *love* my body — pain, illness, and all.

Through yoga, I began to also believe that there is a God or a source or energy (whatever one may call it) because I could *feel* it. Yogananda called it the *ocean* and said that we are the *waves*.

I learned that if life is to be truly lived, we need to strike a balance between our higher aspect — the spiritual — as well as the material, enlightenment being the perfect balance between the two. I now believe that disease is the body's way of saying, *"Look, something's out of balance."* Change the body, you change the mind; change the mind and the body changes.

One of my yoga teachers, Noah Heney, once told our class, "Yoga is for everyone. Practice it to stretch and tone your body, to find inner peace, and maybe even enlightenment."

I would add *heal* to this list, for it encompasses all.

You, more than anyone else, deserve your love and affection.
~The Buddha

A House for My Soul

Nance Thacker

In 1968, I was an anorexic 16 year-old gymnast, dreaming of Olympic gold, but cast adrift when my gymnastics coach and mentor, Mr. Stewart, left our school. With his departure, the greatest support I had of my beloved sport ended.

For the next few months, I attempted to teach myself armed with reel to reel tapes supplied by the school, of a reedy gymnast effortlessly performing her skills. In my case, however, I trained in an empty gymnasium with an unforgiving, linoleum-covered concrete floor to cushion my landings. With no one left to guide me, my frustration mounted. I missed the encouragement of my coach who had made me feel I could do anything; even when my attempts fell short of my goals, he would always celebrate my efforts. Discouraged, I soon quit.

When one is young, low self-esteem can cloud anyone's mind but, on top of this, I was plagued with anorexia. From my perspective, my current life mirrored what my "slim" future had to offer, and a fear of not being adequate enough to rise up and meet the challenges of life just magnified my anxiety within. I wanted desperately to succeed but wanted to become invisible, as well, so I turned to running, weight training and stretching to burn away my incessant, negative thoughts. Movement focused my mind, blocking out negative chatter; power over my body gave me a false sense of control.

One day, I happened to stumble upon a yoga program on TV featuring Kareen Zebroff, a teacher with a childlike sense of play. The work was serious, but she took herself lightly, and she and her crew behind the camera laughed often. She inspired me to explore movement through yoga, and my strong kinesthetic sense to refine movement became my guide. After several weeks of practicing, I began to feel much more empowered and devoured such books as Jess Stearn's *Yoga, Youth and Reincarnation* and Van Lysbeth's *Yoga Self-Taught* to learn more.

My overwhelming compulsion to eat minuscule amounts still existed, however, as I did not yet comprehend the ahimsa aspect of yoga: practicing nonviolence to oneself and others. Each morning as I stepped onto the scale, the numbers seemed to drop further than the day before, until my weight plummeted beyond the target of ninety pounds that I had set for my barely five foot frame. Alarmed, but caught in a groove of self-destructive behavior, I could not stop my downward spiral toward the abyss.

Not much was known about anorexia in those days. The decline of the renowned singer, Karen Carpenter, and her death in 1983 from complications due to anorexia, ultimately brought it to the forefront of public awareness. All I knew, in the early '70s, was that I was battling a conflict within myself that consumed all aspects of my being: mind, body and spirit. The vantage of the "observer," cultivated by my yoga practice, at least gave me some solid ground from which I could witness my predicament with some detachment and gain some understanding. That I could recognize and acknowledge my emotions and strive for clarity was my saving grace.

When an appendicitis attack required my hospitalization and surgery, it was with a sense of relief that I surrendered to both. It was the eve of my 18th birthday. As I lay on the table observing the anesthetic being injected into my arm, surrendering to unconsciousness felt like a welcome death.

"Oh, my God — she's so *skinny*," I heard the nurses exclaim as they lifted me into bed after the surgery. It was the first time my thin, naked body had been exposed to anyone. The shock in their voices pierced through my resurfacing consciousness and knocked me into a whole new reality; I could ignore my problem no longer. That day, I resolved to move in the direction of health and healing — to throw away the scale, the mirrors, and my fears of failure and the future.

"*I will eat to feel well*," I promised myself. As I convalesced, being perceived of as fragile — and treated as such — repulsed me, so I decided to become as strong as my practice had been showing me I could be. On the mat, I would do only the most fundamental poses in order to heal and to regain my strength and stamina. "Patience" became my mantra, "the present" my new place of residence, "awareness" my new therapist. My goal became not only physical health but also the integration of my body and mind, spirit and speech.

With this new intention, I became curious about the profound teachings that Kareen hinted lay beneath one's yoga practice, and felt empowered to liberate myself from the tyranny of my "monkey-mind." My exploration of meditation and philosophy naturally evolved and, with my deepening practice, my wisdom and health did, as well. I came to realize that there is no such thing as "perfection" — including the perfection in body and life that my 16 year-old self sought to attain so I could finally declare, *"I have made it!"* Just an illusion, as well.

My soul was yearning to feel the state where love and wisdom and grace and compassion exist, where neither fear nor judgment resides. To arrive closer to this state, I had needed to delve deep into my fears and judgements to know their nature and, in so doing, dissolve the power they held.

~ ~ ~

Some view anorexic behavior as a subconscious form of rebellion against cultural messages and expectations about what it is to be a woman in our society. Hypersensitive to the deeds, words and the very thoughts of others, perhaps I could not stomach nor digest certain life experiences and aspects, resulting in my appetite for life being lacking.

The huge contradiction I felt between my feelings of isolation and powerlessness in this physical life — versus the vastness of the spirit — made life all the more difficult.

Years later, during my studies to become a Shiatsu therapist, I came across the concept of "the body housing the soul," and I realized that my soul hadn't wanted to be in my body — as if it was rejecting this place of residence as being too small and inconsequential to contain the immensity of spirit.

To live this human life is to experience a range of extreme emotions — desire, fear, envy, sorrow, joy, passion, love and rage, which can threaten to overwhelm us. We come into this world and this terrible beauty we call "life" choosing to walk the razor's edge between desire and detachment; yet, once we are here, we spend most of our energy seeking to escape through the diversions and distractions of our mind.

The practice of yoga cultivates my desire not to escape as often, but rather to connect with the "Witness/Observer" part of my mind; the meditative state of spaciousness that occurs during my practice is now a part of my being. It breaks through when I am giving healing sessions or spontaneously arises during or after periods of intense emotion, confusion or challenge.

It is the calm awareness beyond all things, the quiet timeless place within where the "knowing" exists. From that state, the perfection of each moment is realized, and with it, the knowledge that I am spirit manifest and consciousness evolving.

As are we all.

Yoga removes the illusory veil that stands between us
and the animating force of life.
~ Donna Farhi

The Big Picture

Sonny Rollins

As a child, I was brought up in the usual Christian church and I always had a sense of self-worth, I always had a sense of conscience that talked to me, and I always knew there was more to reality besides the obvious. That feeling has propelled me through life.

At different periods, during crisis situations, I depended more and more on my inner self, my inner voice, and I started to become aware of the "Big Picture." So I feel I was meant to become involved with yoga. It was just inevitable. And here's the story of how it came to be.

As I grew up, I did stupid things like we all do. When I was a kid, we lived in an apartment building. My friends and I used to go up on the roof, which overlooked a backyard pathway where people would go from one block to the other. We thought it would be great fun to drop mortars down from the roof and scare people.

On one occasion I did this and dropped a pretty heavy piece

of mortar from the roof. There was a guy walking by down there and it was headed right for him. I realized that if this thing hit him, "that's it" for him, and I really began praying. I think I got really close to God in those few seconds. I began praying hard and strong that this wouldn't hit him — and thank God it didn't. It was my first big, personal encounter with what I consider to be a "guardian angel" or "bigger power" or "great spirit" or whatever you want to call it. But it was the way that I began to get to know my inner voice.

Later on, in my early twenties and as a professional musician in New York, I got into some other stupid things. This time, I got involved with drugs. One day while I was with my friend Bud Powell, the great pianist, we went up on the roof of a tenement building to get high. After Bud injected his shot of heroin, he passed out, and I mean *passed out!*

I'd never been in that situation before with *anybody*. It was just the two of us there. Since I was younger than Bud, I was in better physical shape and I felt responsible for him. Bud was completely out and I began thinking, "*Suppose Bud expires here, I would be responsible.*" That was another time when I started praying hard again, and my prayers were answered; Bud began coming back to consciousness. Extreme crises like those really make you aware of the seriousness of life.

I became strengthened in my beliefs and I started seeking out books and literature about self-development and the spiritual path. I also joined the Rosicrucian Order, which is one of those metaphysical organizations. Then, in the mid-1950s, I read the book that completely turned me around: *Autobiography of a Yogi*, by Paramahansa Yogananda.

As I was reading it, I thought, *"This is what I've been looking for."* It clarified so much about what's possible in this life. Yogananda was a beautiful personage. I even have my original copy of the book, though the pages are quite worn.

I was ready for the yogic experience. I never knew there were so many types of yoga — prana yoga, karma yoga, raja yoga— until I discovered the writings of Swami Sivananda, another great spiritual teacher whose books I had started reading.

In 1967, I traveled to India and stayed at an ashram not far from Bombay. The residing swami was Swami Chinmayananda. I stayed there about four months and studied the early yogic teachings: the Upanishads, Vedanta and the basic teachings of Patanjali, the author of the ancient *Yoga Sutras*. During my stay, one of the things I confided to the swami was that I had trouble meditating in the conventional manner. He counseled me that playing my horn was a form of meditation, and that my personal yogic path was karma yoga — dedicating my life to working selflessly without seeking the fruits of such work.

It was all coming together for me and I was about ready to return home. The whole experience of India was so intense that when I returned to America, I was literally walking on air, something akin to levitation. This condition lasted for a couple of weeks.

Speaking of levitation, I later began meditating and concentrating to the extent that I was able to float, or leave my body, and rise up to the ceiling of my room. This was an exhilarating experience for sure, but I had been warned in India of the distraction of these siddhi powers, which were available as one advanced on the path but were not the goal.

The next sage I would meet on my path was the renowned Indra Devi, a European woman who wrote several books on yoga, principally *Yoga for Americans*. I visited her ashram in Tecate, Mexico. She imparted some mantras to me such as *"Om Siddi Ram"* which I could easily meditate on, and she was a cordial host, a very spiritual soul. She was also a student of the aforementioned Swami Sivananda whose book, *The Complete Illustrated Book of Yoga*, was my textbook. I still have my dog-eared copy.

I practiced whenever I could, every day, to the best of my ability. The whole attitude with which I entered into these poses was one of yogic concentration, and looking back, I think I achieved a higher level of consciousness which may have stayed with me. It had an effect on everything I did — including my music — especially when I was practicing it in a focused, meditative way and not just going through the physical motions of hatha yoga.

Some musicians shared my interests, and there were a few who sought to make that spiritual leap away from our lives as jazz musicians. John Coltrane was one. He and I used to exchange books and always talked about spiritual things. John was almost all spirit.

By the time 9/11 happened, yoga had long been an integral

part of my life. I heard the plane coming in, and the crash, and everything that followed. I'm sure yoga helped me deal with it, because I felt a certain calm and equanimity through it all. I was able to observe everything with a degree of detachment; it wasn't "me" watching everything — I was just there in a third-person kind of way.

Though I lived only six blocks from Ground Zero, there wasn't a lot of structural damage to my house. Instead, there was toxic damage, the result of contaminated material that ended up in the air-conditioning ducts and everywhere else in the building. My wife and I never slept in the apartment again. In the months afterwards, I had to dispose of our belongings, one of them being a rare book on the Bhagavad Gita, by Bhaktivedanta Swami Prabhupada, with great yogic illustrations.

I lost all of the material possessions I had in that apartment — records, music, my piano, books, stage clothes — and I felt aggrieved at the loss. Eventually, I came to realize that material things were really just that — material things. My spiritual practices enabled me to detach from them.

Because of yoga, I feel much more at peace. Of course, I'm not *completely* at peace because I haven't learned it all. I'm still trying to clean up my karma and so on. But I think I'm on the right track, and yoga has helped to define what that track is. I believe in soul, I believe in reincarnation, so I think that I had an opportunity presented to me to get involved in yoga in this life.

I continue to do my asanas, but since the human frame loses its elasticity over time, I now do a more moderate adaptation.

Of course, the breath is everything, and just sitting erectly and breathing correctly will produce desired results. This practice is called pranayama in yoga.

How has yoga helped my music? Having a more informed belief, more assured and accepting, has enabled me to concentrate more deeply and enter into that place where my musical creativity resides. With music, I want to be connecting with the subconscious and be at that place where creativity happens. When playing my kind of music, the idea is to avoid conscious thinking.

Once you really understand the principles of yoga, you can apply them to everything. It's just the way we're supposed to live. Yoga gives you the Big Picture, and when you start thinking about the Big Picture, it impacts your whole existence.

It certainly did mine.

Reflections

Let nothing dim the light that shines from within.
~ Maya Angelou

Journey to Myra

Sabine Gifford

Many people come to yoga when they reach a crisis in their life, when trauma has taken hold, and when they no longer know where to turn. Twenty-six years ago I was a child in crisis. One of those children who have nowhere to turn.

I share my type of journey with many. Some have just started along their journey, some of us are well on our way, but all of us hope to eventually reach our destination. It is a destination of healing from something which seems to tear our chakras from their core, a destination of healing from the darkness, healing when the light at the end of the tunnel seems unreachable.

My journey began 1984, while I was living in rural West Germany with my parents and two brothers. I was an adventurous and energetic child. That is, until I emerged from my toddler years and reached the ripe old age of six. That's when my grandmother's boyfriend began sexually abusing me.

It would be many years before I'd find the light of yoga.

~ ~ ~

When one is betrayed by a person they are supposed to trust and respect, they often begin dissociating — feeling like they are outside of their body and watching from above. I developed a fear of close relationships, as well. For years. Wirh friends, with relatives, with everyone.

The best way I could cope was to be emotionally strong on the outside and to appear to have my life under control. By the time I graduated with a Masters Degree in education, I actually believed that I was functioning well. Newly immigrated and married in the U.S., I felt the future was finally mine — that all was well in my own little world. It was something I *had* to believe. It was my survival tactic, a way I could feel a part of the "norm."

As I'd soon learn, this survival tactic was but a thin, fragile shield.

~ ~ ~

For a couple of years, I dabbled in yoga for the neck pain I'd developed during my long hours of studying in school. I didn't continue with the yoga, but after I moved to the U.S. to marry Brian, the love of my life, he wouldn't stop raving about how it could help me. "It helped my injured back, and what is good for me can't be bad for you!"

At first, I listened to him just because it promised me a good workout. Also, I had just moved, and not knowing anyone except Brian, and not authorized to work without a "green card," I was bored out of my skull.

When I tried the yoga videos Brian had bought for himself however, they were tortuous, especially because I couldn't manage to both watch the sun salutations and do them at the same time. It made me question whether I was even meant to do yoga! But practicing with the tapes did help me maintain some sanity during that difficult, new period of my life.

Eventually, Brian tried to get me to do yoga with him — at the hotel where I worked. "I need you to go to the class with me because, without you, I won't be allowed to go," he tried convincing me. So I listened to him. He was the best thing that had ever happened to me and had worked with me through thick and thin, a best friend who had been by my side for years. I would trust him once again, and the class would change the course of my life.

"Yoga is not about what you can *do*; it's about how your body *feels* — what makes you feel good. There is no competitiveness in yoga," the teacher explained. I practiced for hours over the next few weeks until I no longer wanted to do another asana! Then, one day, in the middle of my practice, I felt a tremendous sensation of bliss. A sense of calm *totally* consumed me, and began a breakdown of my shield, a long-awaited journey to my Self, a dissolving of my lifelong, trauma-based fear. In its place, I became enthralled in the feeling of my body as it moved through three-dimensional space.

When Brian and I moved to Wisconsin a year later for his career change (from being a lobbyist to becoming an environmental educator), we were determined to keep yoga

161

in our lives and began offering complimentary morning yoga classes to our coworkers. During this time, I realized that yoga was becoming a primary factor in my existence and that there was so much more to be explored. It spurred me to go on a focused search for a new yoga teacher, and I found her in Kristie, a young woman full of energy and life who encouraged her students to live every moment to the fullest.

It would be Kristie who would help me slip out of yet another one of the layers that had held me hostage for so long. As she adjusted my asanas, I suddenly felt my body no longer as the "thing" that had been messed with when I was a child, but that it was mine alone. I may stop perceiving it as an empty shell and infuse some life back into it. There were more changes to come.

~ ~ ~

Up to this point, I was very apprehensive about meditating because I thought it meant a "higher power" had a hold on my life. The concept reminded me of being abused and having no choice about it, but I was still curious. Fortuitously, I found Sharon Salzberg's book, *Insight on Meditation,* which took a "not so religious" perspective on meditation quieting the mind, and I decided to give it a try. It was the next step I needed in being able to accept who I was.

In life, I had never been satisfied with myself, what I was doing or how I appeared, but the more I meditated and did asanas, the more I heard my inner voice and came to uncover my true self. *And* started to love not only myself but also the body I was living in. My energy blossomed, my goals became clear and, as much as I had hated yoga in the beginning, I could no longer imagine my life without it.

It was an intense, hours-long, meditation workshop which would be my ultimate test. At the end of it, terrified that I might revert into dissociation, I ran back to my room, hiding in a flood of tears. But several minutes later, I summoned all my bravery to return. "How do you know if you're meditating or just dissociating?" I asked the teacher, afraid to hear the answer since dissociation was exactly what I'd been trying to avoid; how could I meditate if it put me in danger of losing myself again?

His answer, contrary to my expectation, opened me up to a whole new understanding, "Unlike dissociation, where your mind is trying to *leave* your body, with meditation you are trying to be fully *there* — *in the moment*. You are in your body experiencing every little piece of the now."

His lesson became the mantra of my life, and I set out to experience more in both my yoga and in my life. Wanting to spend as much time as I could manage in each asana, I now held them, feeling and breathing into every tightness, experiencing any fears that arose. As I felt a greater sense of inner expansion, my confidence expanded, as well.

~ ~ ~

Aside from my fear of dissociating, there had always sat another great fear, one which haunted me for years: that of becoming a parent. Aside from the typical fear of whether I'd even be a good mother, I was petrified of having a little being take over a portion of my body; yet, I was ready to trust that I would be fine and that the presence of new life would be a feeling of beauty, reminding myself of my mantra to experience more, not less. I wanted to be as present for this pregnancy as possible.

Every morning, I'd get up early and retreat to my meditation cushion to fully be with "me" and — I soon realized — to connect with the little being inside of me. I came to love this time that I could consciously spend with our unborn child. It was such an incredible feeling not only to give myself the gift of a full breath, but to share it with another human being. Myra is seven months old today.

~ ~ ~

There is one thing that my abuse never managed to strip away from me, and that was my firm belief that I deserved to find someone special who would understand me and be there for me.

Fortuitously, my husband also lead me to an ancient practice which would allow me to be there for myself, which would empower me, heal my soul, and set my inner child free once again.

Reflections

It is only with the heart that one sees clearly.
~ Antoine St. Exupery

The Road to Compassion

Janet Aschkenasy

My grandmother was 87 when she slipped on our porch and slid from her role as both the family matriarch and guardian of my mother who had debilitating schizophrenia.

Almost overnight, everything my grandmother had been managing so smoothly — the oversized cheque book, the monthly bills, and the insurance and medical care for covering both my elderly grandparents — fell smack into my lap. Ever since Mom left Dad when I was two years old, Grandma had been my other mother. Now I had to be hers.

For some time, my cousin had lived in my grandparents' home and helped out with the bookkeeping and the shopping. For a while, he even administered Grandma's meds. Following my grandmother's hip fracture and subsequent pneumonia in 1999, however, he informed me that he was leaving.

I began to feel like I was falling down an endless well. As the busy managing editor of a monthly financial magazine, I was struggling to both supervise Grandma's care and handle my editor's duties, and was clearly in over my head.

"You need to do something life-changing," one of my supervisors bluntly told me when I begged for time off, and recommended a Catskill Mountains health spa that he and his wife had dreamed of visiting themselves..

Little did I know the great effect his words would have on my life. Six months later, when Grandma succumbed to her ill health — and in the midst of my particularly black mood following her death — I found myself at the spa for a Christmas weekend yoga workshop.

One moment I was doing Mulabhanda, a perineal "lock" pose, holding my pelvis rock solid as my chest glided toward the sky, and the next thing I knew, a powerful bolt of ecstatic energy moved like a shot from my heart to my heels. I was awestruck! *"How could such a simple way of moving the body engender such a remarkable change in mood?"* I asked myself.

After class, I ran after the teacher, Christopher Ken Baxter, to learn more. I knew nothing about the different schools of yoga, and Christopher was one of the founders of the Kripalu Center for Yoga & Health. "You need to practice yoga in New York," Christopher declared. Given my remarkable experience in class, I decided to take heed.

Once back home, I found my way to Rasa Yoga Studio, a humble west-side-of-Manhattan studio that offered me the opportunity to investigate the hidden power of sound through chanting. Singing had always been something of a secret love for me, and Rasa Yoga used humming and chanting to accompany a slow and soothing asana flow, with sound and breath in tandem, to support a flowing yet deliberate movement of sequences. Sometimes the sound in the room was discordant; other times, the place rang with a hypnotic sea of vocals that fostered a profound sense of space and harmony.

Best of all, perhaps, in those lonely days when I was moving everything out of the home I grew up in — my grandparents' sprawling and overstuffed three-story house — sorting through Grandma's things and selling what we didn't need, I was able to go to classes, curl over onto my mat any time I needed to, and cry my heart out in the company of friends.

For the next five years, my life was all about the yoga studio. I took its first certified teacher training program, began volunteer teaching AIDS patients at a community health clinic soon thereafter, and found that Rasa's gave me some earth to stand on during this heartbreaking period when I also had to find Mom a new place to live (and designate someone besides me to help look after her).

While my life wasn't completely a blissful blur of classes, my sister said that I glowed. In retrospect, I think I was learning to love myself and it was drawing to me what I wanted or needed most — including the ability to work at home in New York several days a week rather than commuting three hours a day to my editorial job in Greenwich, Connecticut. I never even requested the change of location; my boss — as tough a manager as you could ask for — simply offered!

And, for the first year or so after beginning to practice yoga religiously in early 2000, a number of sticky job problems worked themselves out without my feeling as though I had lifted a finger.

It was also heady and exciting to move from being a fledgling student to volunteer teacher — frequently assisting my own teacher. I'd spend several summers at Rasa's countryside yoga retreat in New Hampshire, happily helping out with students and with the sprawling organic vegetable farm on-site.

The honeymoon though, would sadly come to an end, as Rasa Yoga's Manhattan studio would close. Two friends and business partners who had been running things there for over ten years were now embarking on different paths. In many ways, the closure resembled my family's dissolution when I was an infant, and I would be tested on how well I could maintain the sense of equanimity I had developed for months on the mat. While Rasa had its share of problems, it had served as a unique place of healing and anyone entering our classroom could feel the walls singing with something else — the years we had bombarded the studio with gratitude, devotion and sacred intent were present, or at least that's how it seemed to me.

Then, just as I hit age 44, in 2005, my new romantic interest, Sing Si, unexpectedly died, and my grief exploded. For months, I hardly slept, I lost weight, and I had difficulty focusing on my work and my care-giving responsibilities for Mom. Fortunately, she weathered the storm very well. I did not. I was a freelance journalist who feared for my career. I pushed, I forced, and I managed, but I hated every minute of it. Many times, I even asked myself whether I was equipped to continue teaching my own weekly classes and those for my the AIDS patients. I took a couple of months off from teaching, in early 2006, and wondered if I would ever return. I felt nauseous, I felt dizzy, I felt the disconnected lag of sleeplessness, and I became largely disinterested in crucial things like my bills and bank balance.

One fateful Tuesday, I decided that something had to give. I forced myself out of bed early that morning and, with new purpose, hobbled over to the yoga class at The Breathing Project.

My teacher, Zack Kurland, who had taught me anatomy and vinyasa, took a long look at me.

"You're stronger than you think," he said. He then reminded me that change is not always comfortable, though the urge to stay comfortable is probably one of the greatest hooks there is.

~ ~ ~

Looking back, I think I had become angry with myself for crashing. I hadn't accepted my feelings of loss around my beloved sanctuary, Rasa Yoga, nor around my grandmother who had passed away months before. And the unexpected death of my friend, Sing Si, was the last straw.

I tried to control these feelings, to stay "comfortable," but they kept coming up as bodily discomforts that kept me locked me inside my suffering. Then, I'd berate myself in a *what the hell is wrong with you?*" sort of way. I was not even practicing

171

ahimsa, the tenet of yoga, on myself.

Years ago, when I resented my Mom's disease for robbing me of part of my childhood — the part with a functioning mother in it — I was often angry at her illness. I now know this reflected the unreasonable expectations I bore toward my *own* weaknesses.

I now realize that without looking hard at another person's vulnerabilities, seeing yourself in them and opening your heart, there can be no self-love and no love of the spirit that connects us all. Through yoga, I eventually learned how to look from a place of self-acceptance, which has helped both myself and those I love.

Recently, at dinner, with some of my friends and me, Mom began fidgeting nervously with her hair and dress. Ironically, I'd been engaging in the same habits a little earlier. But, instead of criticizing her as I might have done in days gone by, I just took her hand and whispered, "You know what they say, Mom. The apple doesn't fall far from the tree!" Her smile could have melted an iceberg.

Taking yoga "off the mat" has melted mine.

Reflections

Do not consider your body a mere lump of flesh.
It is a noble instrument... God dwells in the body.
~ Swami Muktananda

Sweating the Big Stuff

Robert Knoss

I remember my very first yoga class well. It was in April, 2003. A friend had raved about the energizing effects of hot yoga where a series of asanas are performed in a studio heated to more than 100°F. *"Sounds great,"* I thought. I was in for the biggest surprise — and healing — of my life. And an answer to my deepest prayers.

That first class, however, I had no idea hot yoga would help save my life. All I knew was that a stunning heat blasted me instantly, I couldn't manage any of the poses, and although I was sitting most of the time (with streams of sweat pouring onto my towel), I was totally exhausted and gasping for air. Sitting at the back of the room, I thought nobody had noticed.

At the end of the class, the lithe instructor switched off his microphone, strode to the back of the room, and asked whether I was okay. Catching my breath, I pointed to the fresh, fourteen-inch long scar across my stomach, and told him that my recent abdominal surgery to remove a chunk of my cancerous liver was probably the reason I couldn't keep up. He looked at me, shook his head, and said, "Frankly, I don't think you should be here."

I went back two days later. And many more times after that.

Why on earth would I go back into that hell to humiliate and exhaust myself? Against the advice of the instructor? I guess, initially, there were two compelling reasons. First, although the heat was draining me to a great extent, my body seemed to crave it; after weeks in an intensive care unit with up to eight intravenous drips simultaneously washing chemicals into my veins, twisting in poses while profusly sweating appeared to be an effective way of eliminating these toxins. Second, I was blatantly confronted with how much I had neglected my body and allowed it to rot away.

Students around me were able to bend themselves into beautiful shapes with ease and it was clear they had the harmonious relationship with their bodies that I must have lost ages ago. And the studio had mirrors, so I was forced to look at the wreck that I now was, such as witnessing how I wasn't even able to stand on one leg while resting the other foot in my hands during a mild forward bend.

I'd later realize that being flexible in mind, instead, is the actual point of yoga, but after dealing with cancer and a body that had truly fallen apart, admiring the physical poise of others inspired me to continue.

As I became more familiar with the yoga series, I began to know the inticracies of my body. For the first time, I noticed the small oddities of my skeletal structure and began to listen internally to discover what I needed to do to contort into various asanas. Muscles that I previously thought were outside the range of my control slowly started to cooperate, and I discovered how to work with my breath and how to get my body to bend on an exhalation just a bit farther than I had deemed possible before.

All of this was powerful stuff. My over-analytical mind that had managed to recklessly abuse my body for so many years all of a sudden delved into the marvels of subtle muscle contractions and minute movements of ligaments and bones.

After several months, I felt much better in my body and mind and became quite curious about the "whole" of yoga. The physical exercises had been a good starting point, opening both my joints and mind, but the philosophy of yoga now also compelled me and I was introduced to my next wonderful teacher at just the right time. This one taught Iyengar yoga.

What did he first teach us? Ironically, the universal principles or *yamas*, the first of which is "ahimsa." Generally translated as *kindness, nonviolence*, and *compassion*.

"Basic stuff," I naively thought. *"Every philosophical school has a code of ethics."* When I actually took time to study the all-encompassing definition of non-violence — which starts first and foremost with how we treat *ourselves* — it dawned on me how far removed I'd become from even the very first of the basic principles. If I had carelessly violated my own body for years, how likely was I to treat others, and the environment, with consideration and respect? Hmmm.

So, up on the bookshelf, next to my newly-acquired anatomy

books, went books about Indian philosophy as well as those on Ayurvedic and Chinese medicine. I had quit my job in banking several months before to study nutrition and to recover, and this valuable time allowed me the hours to soak it all up — and to do more yoga!

The prognosis for my type of liver cancer is pretty bleak, the two-year survival rate being a single-digit percentage number. I'm now in my seventh year post-diagnosis, however, travel widely, and have plans for many more years of my wonderful, new-found life.

And, once in a while, I go back to that hot, sticky studio to sweat it all out. After the class, when everyone is leaving, I remain on my mat and quietly celebrate the "wet-noodle state" with some extra forward bends and spinal twists.

At the very end, before I get up to leave, I gently bow my sweaty head. And give thanks.

Reflections

One learns through the heart, not the eyes or the intellect.

~ Mark Twain

Following the Mystic Signs

Tracey Ulshafer

I was never a very active child. I was more of a cerebral kid who preferred reading and playing with dolls to a game of tag or kick-ball. But I didn't really mind because sports weren't something that I wanted to do anyway.

In high school, I couldn't understand why I had to take gym class, so I always chose the skill-based choices like paddle-tennis or archery — ones that had an intellectual bent. Because I always did well, nobody pushed me to do anything more physical.

And, I was the type of girl who chose to lounge in my bikini by the pool (suntanning instead of playing water sports with my friends) and who would accompany friends to ski hills usually just for the bus trip — waiting in the chalet for them to return while I drank cocoa by the warmth of the fire! I was fine with all this; it was just who I was.

But, when I was just 16, my life changed drastically when a severe car accident left two of my thoracic vertebrae fractured. Because I was young, the doctors said that I'd healed quickly and were very pleased with my recovery. I thought nothing of it at the time and continued a relatively inactive physical lifestyle. Soon after college, however, I became overwhelmed with the stress of a middle management office job. And the consequences were beyond my imagination.

By the time I was 27, arthritis had developed in my back and I was popping about eight pills a day just to deal with the pain. My back would often "go out" for two to three days just by my cleaning the house, and the doctors were amazed that I was able to function as well as I could. (They wondered why I didn't have more serious disk problems but that day came too). I also acquired chronic sinus infections and allergies and, on a personal level, I was in an awful relationship that I was completely attached to and utterly unwilling to let go of.

To make matters worse, I was the type of person who would not take any responsibility for the things that were happening to me. But when a close friend suggested that I try yoga, I thought, "Why not?" I'd tried the physical therapy route several times to no avail, and I'd joined a gym twice and never went back because it just made me feel worse about myself. Chiropractic care, acupuncture and even doing simple stretches at home never did the trick for me either.

I decided, "Okay, this is it — if *YOGA* doesn't work, I'll consider surgery." I wasn't sure what to expect, as I had a limited understanding of what yoga really was and, truthfully, I don't think that I even enjoyed it much after the first class!

But something made me return again and again.

And lo and behold, one day, the most amazing thing happened. Somewhere within the first two months of doing yoga only once a week, I began feeling better — I gained more strength and flexibility in my body than I had ever felt before! Encouraged, I cut back my medication to one or two pills a day.

As I continued to gain more flexibility in my body, my intuition followed. I heard it loud and clear, and it inspired me to make more small but important changes in my life. Firstly, I realized it was time to take responsibility for my own life and I found the courage to leave the bad relationship that I was in. Secondly, I realized that if I didn't quit my current corporate job, the stress was going to further manifest in my body, creating even more problems. My grandmother was born with polio, and my whole life I had watched her live in a wheelchair. Deep down, I knew that if I didn't make some changes immediately, I might be sitting beside her one day. It scared me to death.

Ironically, in the midst of working through these changes, and after one particularly stressful and physically-demanding day at work, a disk herniated in my neck, pinching a nerve and rendering me immobile and in more pain than I'd ever felt before. I took it as a final sign that I needed to step up my plans to leave the corporate world.

~ ~ ~

If truth be told, I had been stalling. After all, the solid money that I was making and the medical benefits that accompanied it were very nice. It wasn't going to be easy leaving them behind.

Also, I'd been working for this company for twelve years and had made lots of good friends there; it was very comfortable. But once I awakened to the reality that I was causing myself harm and that I had to change this behavior, I had to trust my newly-awakened inner self.

I heeded my yoga teacher's encouragement to enroll in massage therapy training, worked with my neck injury, and took the minimal amount of medication the doctor would allow. And I practiced yoga regularly — against the doctor's suggestion, I may add! I recovered in a record amount of time, then graduated with ease.

It took me nearly two years to leave the corporate world entirely, but after my neck healed, I left the middle-management job, finished massage school, and launched into yoga teacher training one week later.

~ ~ ~

Many people come to yoga for physical healing, and many find their intuition heightened, as was mine, but there was yet another key benefit that revealed itself to me. An astounding, beautiful benefit that may have come from my staying with the journey. An entrance into a level of spirituality that I would never have ever imagined would enter my life.

It's funny how it happened, considering my religious beliefs and background. My parents, being a Jewish and Methodist mix, thought it was best if we made up our own minds about there being a God or "Spirit," so we neither went to church nor synagogue. Since I had no vantage point, I just figured that this type of spirituality was something I would never have in my life. I believed there was a "higher power," but that was about the extent of my belief system. Not long into my teaching yoga to others, however, I *felt* this higher power. Like everything else on my yogic path, I suppose it just arose in its own time.

One evening, at the end of an intensive class, while sitting in Lotus with my hands in prayer pose and waiting for my students to come out of savasana, I began talking to Spirit — just out of the blue. I thanked it for all the blessings in my life, including all of my students whom I named, one by one.

I don't know whether it was the deep stillness of my mind, my heart chakra opening through this profound practice of gratitude, or a combination of the two, but I suddenly felt completely connected not only to Spirit but also to everyone else who walked through the doors of the yoga studio. And to everyone I share space with on this planet! I'd heard about such unity and love, but now I was actually feeling it first-hand.

As tears streamed down my face, there was a joy in my heart the depths of which I could never have thought possible. Something huge was shifting in me, something that had been waiting in the wings for years.

~ ~ ~

There is little more to say. Love had entered the picture, and I would never be the same again. I realized I no longer needed my self-pity and I replaced it with consideration for everything as a whole; compassion for others now replaced my previously selfish self. From this new space, I began to honor my body and just breathe. I allowed myself to be human, to make mistakes and to move at my own speed, knowing that wherever I am is exactly where I am meant to be.

Today, I never need to take pain medication for my back and only gets colds when I stop listening to my body and push myself to extremes. And, whenever I fall into those all-too-human traps that deal with ego and not honoring one's truth, I have the awareness to recognize them and steer the other way.

I hope that others, in times of difficulty, see me as their torch, a light to guide them along their yogic journey. A journey dotted with mystic signs which lead one to their greatest light... their true self.

Reflections

Adapt yoga to the individual, not the individual to the yoga.
If you can breathe, you can do yoga.
~ Sri. Krishnamacharya

A Life Worth Living

Martha Patt

On August 20, 1984, I was diagnosed with multiple sclerosis. It was the last blow of a series of inexplicable symptoms starting in 1979: a blind spot in my right eye, my right hand going limp for two months, weakness along the rest of my right side, and an odd tightness in my torso. Unbeknownst to me, it would be a new chapter toward a more fulfilling life.

But on this day of the final chapter of my old life, all I knew was that this time I woke up with a weak *left* arm, tension, numbness a loss of sensation from my diaphragm to my feet, and persistent pain from my knees to my toes. I could hardly walk.

After my diagnosis, I was not sure if I had the strength and determination to go on. I was 26 years young and my previous life challenges paled in comparison. Inside of me was a monster buzzing with constant pain; I'd wake in the morning feeling like I was different — an outcast — and that nobody would want to hear about my new reality, I'd go to bed at night thinking, *"What will I do if my legs do not work in the morning?"*

"Maybe I could cut my legs off and the pain will go away," I fantasized. *"Or crawl to the bathroom if my bladder calls."* Detachment to my situation became my driving force as I had no choice but to be in the present moment.

At the time, I was living alone and dealing with rejection and despair, as my partner of five years had left. Shortly after my diagnosis, I connected with the Northern California chapter of the National Multiple Sclerosis Society (NMSS), becoming an official member of the "club." My first telephone conversation with one of their counselors ended in tears after they told me what to expect from MS: severe fatigue, depression, cognitive issues, and a host of other disabling symptoms.

Following that early morning conversation, I drove to work feeling as though I had a meaningless past and perhaps a meaningless future, as well. After reading the literature sent from the NMSS, I learned that nearly 66% of Multiple Sclerosis (MS) patients need to use some device to help them walk — they require a cane, walker or a wheelchair just five years after their diagnosis. This was not the life I had imagined in my little-girl dreams.

After attending my first support group meeting for the "newly-diagnosed," I decided *not* to become part of the majority who need assistance — I determined, rather, to be part of the rare 34% that can still walk as regular people do. But I was living alone, was laid off from my job, and I had a severely diminished sense of self.

That June, 1985, I gave myself three years to see if I could make it to my 30th year on this planet and *then* determine if life was worth living. And one day, the universe gave me an answer.

While continuing my distance swimming and counseling sessions, I had an epiphany: All of my previous exacerbations occurred whenever I placed myself in stressful, self-destructive situations. Or if I took on the concerns of others. Or when I was living an illusionary life full of fear, feeling like I had neither purpose nor control. I saw that if I could *instead* direct my life in a healthy, meaningful and *conscious* manner, I could prevent my MS exacerbations.

After years of ignoring books, I now found that I devoured ones associated with Eastern philosophy, and I learned such ideas as: *"uncertainty being the fertile ground of pure creativity,"* and *"the unknown is the field of all possibilities"* — from Deepak Chopra's book, *The Seven Spiritual Laws of Success*, and I embarked on a personal mission to do something big with my life.

Living with MS seemed to offer much uncertainty about the unknown, but maybe my illness could offer me new possibilities? I decided to let go of all preconceived notions as to who I was *supposed* to be. I found a new career (with the California Department of Rehabilitation) where I became busy with my job, and I searched for balance in life for my creative and logical mind. Swimming laps kept my legs moving (the water being very soothing to my constant, throbbing pain), and drawing classes offered much pleasure to the right side of my brain.

Then yoga re-entered my life. I remembered the simple asanas that I'd enjoyed at a yoga class a couple of years earlier, and I launched into a simple routine of asanas, pranayama and meditating at home each day, directing breath to my physical discomfort within. Relief visited the chronic pain in my legs and calmed my anxious mind, replacing the discomfort with a sense of spiritual well-being. *Vira* is the Sanskrit word for hero or warrior, and simple asanas, like Virasana, as they stretched and massaged my spine and limbs, allowed me to look deep inside myself and find my strength within.

Learning the discipline to find fresh meaning in my life and to create new dreams, my hope returned. Pain seemed to momentarily sink into the earth almost as if it could be breathed smoothly away and, as yoga did not have any of the negative side effects of the drugs prescribed to me, I made my practice a daily part of my life.

My journey became even more clear when I met my future husband, Bill Patt. At the time, Bill and I were both pursuing a second college degree and a meaningful career path. It was a friendship like I'd never experienced before; between our work and school, Bill and I would meet at small cafes in San Francisco or Berkeley, see movies or share our thoughts on life. Not sure the relationship could survive my disability, however, I kept detached to the outcome.

One time, I asked Bill what he might want to do when finished his schooling. To this day, I remember his profound response: Bill said he wanted "to save the world."

Initially, I thought, *"What about the house with the white picket fence?"* And, *"Don't you want to be successful in our business world?"*

Then I thought, *"How selfish of me. He's a grand visionary!"*

It led me to think, *"maybe I have something to offer this world, too."*

And I *did* have something to offer. Right under my nose. In 1994, after twelve years of practicing yoga alone, I realized I was meant to share my yogic experience with the MS community.

At the time, I had been studying for nearly five years with Swami Sitaramananda at the Sivananda Yoga Vedanta Center in San Francisco. With Bill's encouragement and support, I organized with the ashram and the local chapter of the NMSS, a one day yoga workshop for the MS community. It was the first small step to recognizing my real purpose in life. When nine people with MS came with wheel chairs, canes and walkers, to experience our offering, the excitement I felt was beyond words. I had found my dharma.

From that point on, whenever given the opportunity, I taught yoga to the MS community through various functions offered by my local NMSS chapter. Thankfully, opportunities kept arising as more of the MS community heard about the calming powers of the practice.

My belief that a large segment of my colleagues would want to learn it was confirmed in early 1998, when I hooked up with an Integral yoga teacher, Janet Piggins, and we began our first MS yoga class series where Janet offered simple chair yoga emphasizing body and breath awareness. Interest in the program was beyond what our chapter had ever imagined possible, and because of the great feedback we obtained from our many students — how this gentlest of yoga helped them find comfort and strength — we continued the program for nearly six months.

Since then, I've worked with many renowned MS yoga teachers, such as Eric Small, in workshops around San Francisco Bay. It is most gratifying and satisfying: helping the northern California chapter of the NMSS train local yoga instructors how to effectively work with the MS community.

Today, after more than twenty years of living with MS and practicing yoga daily, I prefer not to focus on my previous life without this illness, but rather on how living with MS and yoga has opened up my heart and mind.

I have truly found a life worth living.

Reflections

Yoga is the restraint of the thought-waves of the mind.
~ The Yoga Sutras of Patanjali

Freedom Beyond the Palms

Lorraine Gane

et go of the past and have no expectations of the future, purrs
the tall, lanky instructor to eleven of us — four men and
seven women of all ages, shapes and sizes — as we lie
motionless on our backs in "corpse" pose.

"*As the mind wanders, bring it back to this moment, this breath...*"
he continues, in a soft Tennessee drawl. I try to focus on inhaling
and exhaling from my abdomen.

It is the fifth day of my week-long stay at the Sivananda
Ashram Yoga Retreat, on Paradise Island, in the Bahamas. Try
as I may, my attention is waning, moving to the aqua sky and
swaying palm trees framed in the window. And to my first day's
arrival...

*As I step off the boat that ferried me from Nassau to the ashram's
dock, I am greeted by the sweet aromas of lovely flowers. Walking
down the path toward the reception area, my eyes are bathed in the
lush greens of overhanging coconut trees, avocado bushes and various
other exotic plants. My room, though small and rustic, looks out through*

197

swaying palms to brilliant aqua water and white sandy shores...

I just barely hear the instructions, *"wiggle your toes,"* and stir from my daydreaming, sit up with the others, and chant *OMMMMMMMMM* — said by ancient yogis to be the vibration of the universe.

Soon, the instructor has us building our "prana" or life force via "kapalbhati breathing," inhaling and exhaling from our abdomen in quick pumping contractions. After the second round of forty pumps, my head feels weightless, once again floating out the window, this time to the white-capped ocean waves.

"We are now going to salute the sun," the teacher declares loudly, cutting into my ocean fantasy once again. He then takes us through a series of leg, arm and body movements that have us breathing heavily by the end of six rounds.

I have not come here solely for the exercise, although my body badly needs it. I have come to slow down and to take a break from a highly stressful period due to the death of my fiancé from cancer. Having developed a bad head-cold and possible ulcer, coming to the Sivananda retreat would turn out to be the perfect place for my healing...

After a short rest on the floor, we are guided into shoulder stands, hip bends, the *cobra* and *locust* asanas, and half-a-dozen other maneuvers. The instructor outlines the virtues of yoga and the need to be compassionate with one's self in its physical form. "Yoga means union — union with the self...You have to listen to the body; some days it's loose, some days tight..."

Up until this class, my body has been the latter, a mass of

coiled muscles. Under the impression that any conditioning would help me prepare for yoga, I took aerobics classes three times a week for a month. I discovered in my first yoga session (on a covered wooden platform overlooking Nassau harbor) what a big mistake I'd made: Aerobics *tightens* the muscles; in yoga, you want them *flexible*!

The instructor asks us to sit on our mats and bend forward from our waists. I ready myself in the appropriate position and push downward. My chest moves down a few inches, then stops. I've hit a wall. "Only bend what feels natural to you," offers our young, slim, blond-haired instructor who sits down on his mat, spreads his legs, and effortlessly lowers his chest to the floor.

The following afternoon, during a class on the ocean platform, with a dazzling sun sinking into endless blue, our teacher is a trim, middle-aged woman with a clear, German-accented voice. She guides us swiftly through the postures which seem to take all my effort. "There are 840 asanas — few of them do you go into forcefully…it's a combination of effort and perfect ease that we are striving for," she suggests. My hopes for quick results are dashed when she confides, "Work your legs every day. Within a year, they should be flexible."

~ ~ ~

A wake-up bell rings at 5:30 a.m. Then, by 6 a.m., we are sitting on pillows in the temple — first in silence, then chanting various Sanskrit verses, followed by a lecture by one of the swamis. Asanas run from 8 to 10 a.m., then there is brunch, free time until 4 p.m., more asanas, dinner, and another round of meditation, chanting and lectures.

I am, therefore, relieved one morning when the routine is broken by a walking meditation on the beach. A bit groggy, I make my way down the steps in the pre-dawn darkness, and join a line of slowly-moving bodies, my bare feet sinking in cool, watery sand. We pass the Club Med compound which is usually teeming with half-naked, sunbathing bodies, and move to a grove of Australian pines. I find a space between fellow meditating, shawl-covered bodies and sit cross-legged on the sand.

When our group has assembled, our swami—a pretty, young woman dressed in a beautiful saffron robe and sporting a shaved head — opens the chant. *OMMMMMMMMM* penetrates the air with her clear, sweet voice, and about one hundred of us join in, creating a resonant sound. Above to my right, through the trees, a soft yellow light radiates from above the horizon.

"To act rightly and to live in God is divine life," says the swami, smiling. "You don't say: *Give me a big house and I'll surrender to you!* There are no conditions…"

The swami's words seem to float through me and become part of the sky, the trees, the stillness of the glassy ocean and the cruise ship offshore. For the first time in months, I feel at one with all — spacious, open and released from the tightness I've carried in my body for so long. This deep inner peace lingers as a brilliant sun rises in the east.

Yoga has set me free.

Reflections

*Life is given to you to experience your own creativity and
your own Self in the dignity of its existence.*
~ *Yogi Bhajan*

Between Culture and Spirit

Reema Datta

I have been hearing my mother sing mantra since I was in her womb. She and my grandmothers, who are from India, sang throughout my childhood, mostly while preparing vegetarian meals from scratch, always laced with subtle and tasty Ayurvedic spices. They would sing to Krishna, Sita, Ram, Ganesh and the many other deities all day while cooking, sewing, gardening and even driving.

On Fridays, during Satsang with my parents, I would hear bits and pieces of the *Bhagavad Gita* and, on Sundays, my uncle would read and explain parts of the ancient Sanskrit epic, the *Ramayana*, for the Indian children in town.

While growing up in North America and India, I loved visiting temples and delighted in watching people sing, dance and worship deities, feeling moved by the devotion and humility with which they would act. I savored the wild, mythological plays that explained the teachings of the Vedas, the gods and goddesses, and their many powers and adventures.

Whenever Hinduism or spirituality became confusing, I would turn to my grandfather, 'Bapuji', who lectured on the Gita and Vedas throughout Europe and America and who has written several books about their significance. He has always explained the most complicated teachings in simple and lucid prose.

For example, in the ancient Hindu scripture, the *Bhagavad Gita,* Krishna says, "Fools think that I have form. Any way you wish to reach me, I will return your love with my love." My grandfather would explain this to me as, "We each have our own way of connecting to and describing the Divine, but the form does not matter because all paths lead to the same loving energy, the same God recognized by all faiths."

When I look back on my time in India and with my family, I recall people who were greatly influenced by yoga's philosophy. They cultivated so much trust and faith in the sacred that they remained accepting, loving and composed in the midst of great challenges. This was especially evident in the very poor but spiritually vibrant city of Varanasi where I spent one year living on the banks of the River Ganga. In this busy, overcrowded city, people maintained a divine connection in the midst of chaos, revealing a mystical elegance throughout their daily activities.

As a child, I was mesmerized by the yogic stories and songs and touched by the people's connection to the sacred. By my early twenties, blessed with a strong yogic background, I began practicing asana and pranayama regularly and was soon able to make my practice a personal, moving meditation.

~ ~ ~

The mythology, dance and art that celebrate the Vedas instill a strong sense of the powers around us, which love and protect us and which preserve the positive and destroy the negative. But while engaging in meditative movement, I felt my own power and realized that the magical and mystical powers of God that I celebrated as a child are inside of me too.

It was around this time that I was blessed to meet my first Western yoga teachers. While Indians focus on being aware of and humble to the sacred powers around us, being grateful for life and acting with detachment and love, my first Western yoga teachers emphasized freedom from mental conditioning and living a life directed by one's truth and intuition.

Cultures are beautiful in many ways, but they tend to foster imitation and conformity rather than individuality. Having the strength and vision to move from conformity to individuality was pivotal on my spiritual path — to develop a direct, authentic connection with the sacred within and around me.

In the stillness and solitude of asanas and seated meditations, I was able to tap into my truth and gain clarity into who I am and what I want. Looking inward took great discipline and courage, but I came to realize that the beliefs of my heart were different than the beliefs of the two cultures I grew up in.

As I continued my daily yoga practice, I began to feel the energy of prana — of breath, of life, of spirit — and a "knowingness" emerged from within me. It was a knowing of my strength and potential because I felt them directly through my breath. Instead of someone *telling* me that I was strong and full of potential or my reading it in a book, I *felt* my vibrancy, power and intuitive energy. As the Vedas proclaim, "Only what you feel is real. Believe only what you experience."

My practice also showed me that there is no reason to fear expressing and living my truth. Doors open when we're courageous; we are protected, rewarded and loved when we follow our natural instincts.

Gradually I developed the courage to express and manifest my truth — even if it went against the expectations of the Indian culture I grew up in and the American one in which I lived. Instead of looking for a high paying job, marriage and home, I followed my passion for yoga, music, and exploring spiritual practices. Interested in the shamanic practices of the Brazilian Amazon and also the healing traditions of Africa, Asia and Europe, I travelled to learn these from their source.

What I found amazed me: elements of yoga are found in indigenous cultures throughout the world, not only in sacred dance, meditation and music but also in a broad understanding of nature and the cosmos itself. The ultimate message of these traditions? *Live your truth fearlessly; move from the core of your being, allow your every expression to represent your highest truth and grandest vision.*

~ ~ ~

During my childhood, rituals and scriptures made me aware of how powerful, magical, creative and loving the sacred is. My yoga practice, however, made me conscious of the power that dwells inside each of us and taught me that there is no separation between myself and the Divine. When one is in the splendid state of yoga — in union with spirit, everything becomes possible — there are no limits, there is no doubt nor fear; such negative words and beliefs dissolve.

On the other side of fear is love. Yoga takes me there. Feeling the love, vitality and interconnectedness of all things has helped me to relax and understand that there is nothing to prove. The most important thing is to remain true to ourselves, to listen to and nurture our soul, and to allow our creativity to surface. When we give from an authentic and creative place deep in our heart, what we give to others has a powerful impact.

I've learned that I must start with myself. Instead of searching for peace, joy, and freedom, I must *be* peaceful, joyous, and fearless. My practice showed me that there is no reason to fear expressing and living my truth; we are protected when we stay connected to our intuition and maintain a lifestyle and spiritual practice that honors our natural impulses.

The path of a yogi is to come into one's own experience, allowing knowledge to flow from the inside. This happens when we create a spiritual practice and life that honors our unique mental, emotional, and physical inclinations, following the message of the Gita: *Never lose your self-integrity...find the truth of your highest, innermost existence and act according to this—your true nature—not any outer standard.* It is a message shared by the many indigenous people I have met along my journey.

When we move from the core of our being, we move from the heart of the universe. When I trust the unknown, I move into a realm of emptiness, a place where ultimate reality can be experienced.

It is stated in the *Hatha Yoga Pradipika* that we practice yoga to evolve together. The vision of the earliest yogis was to cultivate balance and harmony within for the purpose of sharing it with their surroundings — all people, plants, animals and spirits. We may begin spiritual practice by focusing on the self, but ultimately we do yoga for others.

May we each create a life that honors our own truth, and evolve both individually and as a humanity.

Reflections

*Yoga is like music...the rhythm of the body, the melody of the
mind and the harmony of the soul create the symphony of life.*
~ B.K.S. Iyengar

Finding Music in the Divine

Neal Arbic

One night, after the rest of my family had gone to sleep, I picked up a book a friend had given me, *Be Here Now*, by Ram Dass. It seemed a strange, old book, with an odd shape — perfectly square — and on the cover was an empty chair encircled by the words, *"Remember. Be here now. Remember. Be here now."*

Inside were pictures from the 1960s of long-haired hippies walking around India. And there I was, an ex-punk from the '80s, stuck in the suburbs. The book seemed to belong to another world, another time.

As I lingered over the pages, it became clear that it was about meditation, yoga and mystic philosophy. The hours came and went. Some words were within drawings and they turned and curved, snake-like, within the lines of drawn pictures. I'd turn the book in all directions to more easily read the sentences. They spoke of another reality — how we are Spirit rather than our bodies, and how our mind creates its own reality.

When I finally put the book down, at 3 am, I felt a profound silence all around. It was as if I'd lived another lifetime within the space of that one evening. I walked over to the sliding glass doors that led out to our balcony and saw my reflection in the glass, my whole body appearing transparent. For the first time, I saw my physical self not as the real *me*, but as a shadow — the shadow of my soul. A shiver ran up my spine.

~ ~ ~

After reading *Be Here Now*, I would practice meditation and yoga once in a while. I thought they both were cool, but thought that things were pretty normal in my life, so I continued my habits of getting drunk and hooking up and breaking up with girlfriends and bands. Then I formed the band that nearly destroyed me: *A Neon Rome*.

The year was 1985. I was 22. The radio was filled with techno pop music, Ronald Reagan was in the White House instigating another Cold War, and it was the decade of music videos and junk bonds. Being a musician, I was drawn into the secret drug culture of the '80s. I was against all things mainstream and commercial. My life was the dark world of the outcast artist. A punk rocker and atheist since the age of 15, I made up my own rules, which meant that I did whatever I wanted.

While Wall Street traded, I slept. When the brokers slept and the streets of the city were quiet and empty, I and an entire underground of young people awoke. In the middle of the night, we'd gather at dance clubs and alleyways in our own world of psychedelic music and drugs.

A Neon Rome took the underground by storm. It was only a few months before we were at its very center. At 22, I had everything I had ever wanted: groupies, drugs and a rock band of my own.

Music magazines phoned incessantly to interview me. When *The New Music Express* called, I told them rock and roll was my religion. When we played a bar, it was packed. In North America, we were compared to Led Zeppelin; in Europe, to the Sex Pistols. The media nicknamed us "Underground Gurus" and "Coolest of the Cool." One paper said, "Give *A Neon Rome* a hit single, and the world will belong to them!" When our first album was released in Europe and Canada, the press raved, "Not so much awe-some as awe-all!"

After a while, I began buying into my own hype and spent less time with the band and more time indulging in sex and drugs. The more I indulged, the hungrier I became, so I had *more* sex and did more drugs. But I *still* felt unhappy and unfulfilled.

Needless to say, I began to spiral out of control. When the rich and famous kill themselves, people can't understand. But I could.

~ ~ ~

You can only play the edge for so long.

One summer day, I walked straight into disaster and I was too stoned to know it. There I was, flying high on LSD, in ripped army boots, striped pants, and my leather jacket, strolling down

Bloor Street in downtown Toronto, listening to The Doors's *Riders on the Storm,* on my Walkman. The street was lined with open-air cafes and the young and rich having their evening drinks. As the skies darkened, a huge storm moved in. Thunder cracked and rain started pouring down in heavy sheets. People in their business suits ran for cover, but not me — I was tripping!

Then I saw it: A cop car. I thought, *"No problem, I'll just walk by."* But as I passed, the cop got out and told me to put my hands up against the car. He searched me and found a large piece of hash and a bunch of LSD. As I sat in the back of his car, it began to dawn on me: I was going to jail.

As I looked through that steel grid separating the back seat from the front, listening to the two cops deciding my fate, I felt terrible. But I got lucky — they let me go. I was so high though, that after getting out and walking away, I actually turned around and asked for my drugs back. The cop just looked at me in amazement and replied, "I can't do that!"

When I rode the streetcar home, every jerk and bump felt like thousands of razor blades cutting through my body, right down to the deepest part of my soul. By the time I got to my apartment, I just fell to the floor and wept. The radio played *The End* by The Doors. The DJ came on and roared, "Can you feel the VIBE — the psychedelic *VIBE?*"

Suddenly it hit me — the pile of BS that was my life. That was *my* line. That was *me* up on stage telling everyone to drop acid and trip out. And here I was, gnashing my teeth in a suffering I had never known before. I clearly saw the emptiness of my whole trip. My self-created religion could not save me now, for it was my very betrayer. It was my Judas, handing me to Rome.

Gripped with grief and anger, I tried to drink myself into denial at the nearest pub. I don't remember much else other than my stumbling out the back door of the club, passing out again in the alleyway, then awakening to the smell of urine from the street people beside me.

When I got up on my feet, what happened was indescribable. If I had to put it into words, I would say it like this: I felt a "presence." Not like angels coming out of the sky or some bright lights dazzling me, but quite the opposite. I felt a moment of profound clarity, a stillness, like God was with me. I didn't actually *see* God, but I did feel a presence.

I had been an atheist for eight years and had lived as if there was no meaning to life, but at this moment, there was no doubt in my mind — the gentle voice I heard was the voice of God: *"This is where it all ends. This is where your life has led you. You know, I never turned my back on you — you turned your back on me. But if you want to, we'll just call everything square from here-on."*

Then, the voice disappeared.

The next moment my girlfriend, Elsie, came out of the darkness. She got me home.

~ ~ ~

Enough was enough. I vowed to take better care of myself. I took fewer drugs and had the band take a break from playing live to finish our second record. Because we were away from the hassle of doing gigs, everyone in the band had time to take up some extracurricular activities. Remembering how good yoga made me feel, early one morning I decided to do some asanas in my room. Then I lay down on my bed for some relaxation and fell into a deep sleep, accompanied by a mystic dream.

North American Indians call it "The Big Dream." It's an unusual dream where you feel wide awake, and the content of the dream changes your life forever.

In the dream, I dreamt that I stole a van. There was a blizzard, and I remember driving through the snow with my guitarist, Evan. He sat in the passenger seat and kept saying, *"This is your lucky day,"* over and over again. Suddenly, I looked down at my hands and feet, and realized that I was chained to everything I had ever stolen. But now these things were in the form of towering ice blue pegs, shaped like frozen devils standing stiff and straight! Then the blue devils were thrown around. And, being chained, I was thrown with them. I had no control.

It was as if I was a rock, an inanimate mineral, going only where I was thrown. One devil was tossed into a lake, and I went in with him. It felt claustrophobic, like waking up inside a buried coffin or being chained to a wild elephant.

Then, suddenly, I was a bird flying high, high up in the sky. I looked down onto the world, and saw that it was covered in seashells, their spiraling tails pointing up at me. It seemed that they were symbolic of people's lives, their destinies — all their actions spiraling to a single fate. I then looked up and saw that I was headed toward a huge black void. It was the most frightening vision that I had ever seen.

As I got closer, a murky mountain loomed above me and I was engulfed. Everything was shades of darkness. I circled around the mountain and saw — at the top — the back of a black figure, his arms held up to the sky with great authority. I did not want to see this man who lived in this world of shadows, but I couldn't leave — I was drawn toward him.

Approaching him, I saw his eyes. They glowed like moonlight, as if he were hollow and filled with a beautiful, soft energy. Though still surrounded by darkness, I was no longer afraid. "*It's Jesus*," I thought, feeling full of light inside.

Suddenly, he started flying upward, and took me with him. We were flying up to a big, radiant light shining far above the gloomy world below. The joy in my heart was indescribable; all the pleasures, power and fame of my world seemed like an old, cheap dream. We crossed the stream of existence, leaving sorrow behind.

Then he flew up quickly, leaving me behind. A million twisted thorn bushes covered the sky like clouds, and I could not reach or even see the light on the other side.

Motionless in the dark, I wondered why I couldn't see anything and felt like I had no body. Then I heard two people talking somewhere. They were saying great things about this man who, no matter how famous he got, always thought about others; no matter how high or how great his success, he never forgot about those who were weaker and needed help.

Then they spoke of *another* man who stole a van and how the police had caught him the very next day. They never mentioned his name. But I knew better.

I woke up terrified. I had never known such fear and horror. Convinced that my dream showed what the afterlife held for me, I knew I had to take action. I started to return everything I'd ever stolen — which was quite a lot. The final things I returned were books I'd stolen from my old high school.

As I left the school, my deed done, the sun broke through the clouds. The winding path that lead me home sparkled, the puddles reflecting the light. I looked up to the sky and there it was — that beautiful sunlight that shines just after the rain.

It was shining on *me*.

~ ~ ~

A few hours later, I went for band rehearsal. No one was around, but the door was unlocked. I went in, sat down and saw a book, *The Yoga Sutras of Patanjali*, on a table. I started to read it and became so engrossed that I couldn't put it down. It was about the various steps of yoga that lead to full enlightenment. Eight long steps. Joe, the owner of the rehearsal space, walked in, saw I was enamored with the book, and insisted, "Take it!" So I did.

That night, I read through the yoga sutras and couldn't understand everything, but it was enjoyable, like *Be Here Now*, the spiritual journey that had started my own. It spoke about the things that one had to do to experience one's soul and that the hindrances to this were lust, hate and attachment. It said that in order to remove these obstacles, one of the first steps was to abstain from violence, lying, and stealing.

I had always regarded the rules of morality as a drab regimen imposed on me by others, but this book revealed them in a whole new light. It had guidelines, like stars in the night sky guiding lost sailors home. A trumpet call sounded in my head, as if someone was pulling back the veil of the physical world and revealing to me the spiritual light, the foundation of it all.

But I felt so far away from that light — lost and afraid. My resolve was firm, *"I will put my life in order!"* My womanizing had to go next, once and for all.

I woke up Elsie and proposed to her.

~ ~ ~

My interest was now turning toward yoga and meditation and, as I got deeper into the spiritual trip, the band seemed more like a hindrance. While the rest of the band members smoked pot, I tried to quit. I just kept on moving further and further away. And, without me behind them, the band had no cohesive direction.

Maybe it was my being away from the bar scene or that I was now living with Elsie, but life seemed a little more peaceful. One night, I even shaved my head — from long, flowing locks to completely bald. It shocked everyone. This was during a time when Bruce McDonald, a renowned Canadian filmmaker, was following the band around, filming our shows — us backstage, my apartment, and so on. He was planning to do a documentary on *A Neon Rome* and had photographers shooting everything, but by the time he'd gotten the money together to finish it, I was on a vow of silence and declined to be in the film.

Funny thing was, I didn't care. Could this have been the big break for *A Neon Rome*? Maybe. But I had already left the building. I'd had enough.

The last straw came the night I got the tape of our band's second record. For at least two years, we had struggled and scraped for every dollar to complete it. I thought that the night the record was finished would be one of the greatest moment of my life — a triumph that would clear the way to even greater things. I had never worked so hard and long or sacrificed so much.

In my apartment that night, I listened to the record in the dark. It was the loneliest night of my life. I felt so isolated and disappointed. All the lyrics were about sex and drugs —*everything* that I had just turned my back on. I felt like I had spent the last four years furiously building a bridge, only to find out that it was to the wrong island. I quit the band and our second album was never released.

~ ~ ~

The last thing to go was my pot-smoking habit. I was on-again, off-again about the whole deal. But gradually, I made rules: no smoking in public, then, no smoking when Elsie was home, and so on.

It was very hard. Sometimes, I would just break down and cry. Other times, I felt like my whole body was on fire; I had to grit my teeth it was so very painful. When I realized sheer willpower wasn't working, I fully embraced yoga and meditation. This helped *a lot*.

After several months, I succeeded in smoking only when I meditated. After a few more months, I found that when I *didn't* get high, my meditations were much better. So ended my pot smoking days.

~ ~ ~

On June 8, 1988, I married Elsie. By now, I was meditating and doing yoga every day. People told me that I looked happier and healthier. I had a much simpler life — no drugs and no groupies, I'd go to the market, read a holy book, meditate.

I had given up fame and I was happy. I had escaped from the drug-ridden underground, and my new life was all the more glorious by contrast with the misery of the old. But I did not escape unscathed. For three years, as my body detoxified, I experienced very bad health. Even today, my short term memory is poor. But of all my drug buddies, I remain the lucky one.

Of the people I hung out with back then, six died in the drug culture, three of whom overdosed. One guy — the centre of our group — hung himself; one contracted AIDS; three girls fell into prostitution; two other guys are still living on the street with serious drug problems. Another friend — who was the nicest and most sane of us all — went to jail.

I was not completely out of danger, yet.

~ ~ ~

That summer, I saw a street poster for a retreat hosted by the Indian yogi from *Be Here Now*... Baba Hari Dass himself.

Baba Hari Dass — or Babaji, for short — lived in California and India, but came to Toronto every year for a week-long retreat. He taught Ashtanga yoga straight from Patanjali's yoga sutras. Still not completely confident in my new way of life, I went to the retreat feeling it would be good for me to meet Babaji and perhaps find validation for my journey.

For the first five days, I didn't speak to him. I never asked a question in class, I just watched. Here was this East Indian man in his sixties, with a long white beard, who stayed completely silent. He hadn't spoken in over thirty years. It was part of his discipline as a yogic monk. To communicate, he wrote on a small chalkboard which he wore around his neck.

On the sixth day, I decided to meet Babaji in private. I started talking, then suddenly began to cry. Maybe it was my Christian upbringing, but I just started to confess everything wrong I had ever done. Weeping at his feet, my face down in my hands, confessing one crime after another, I would just cry all the more. But at the same time, I felt reassured. When I looked up at his face, it was full of compassion. His face was shining. Like the light of heaven in my dream.

At the end of all of this came no sermon, no indoctrination, nor philosophy. He just wrote on his chalkboard: "Forget the past. Just do positive things. Be married. Meditate every day. Get a job. Live a normal life. And play."

At long last, it felt like my mad tailspin had finally come to an end, like a ship coming into a harbor. Babaji's words resolved any doubts I may have had left. If I had met him when I was in the band, I probably would have just regarded him as some old Indian man sitting on a couch. But with all my meditating, I was quite centered, and could feel the purity of his heart.

Over the next fourteen years, he taught me the balanced path between worldly responsibilities and spiritual growth and how those two become one. Babaji spoke a language that came from the heart — I could *feel* it in my heart. Between his teachings and my yoga practice, my life transformed.

~ ~ ~

There is one particular thing that Babaji wrote over and over again. In fact, there's a joke that he's written it so many times, that it must be ingrained on his chalkboard.

"Do your sadhana."

During '89 to '94, my sadhana was in its most traditional state. I would wake up at four in the morning, do forty-five minutes of breathing exercises, an hour of meditation, and an hour of asanas with a twenty minute savasana at the end. I did this every single day.

I studied classical guitar and piano, attended composition classes at the Royal Conservatory of Music, wrote a few string quartets, sketched a small symphony, and volunteered my time at Greenpeace. I lived on a farm beside conservation land and would go for long walks through the valley.

In November of '89, I started volunteering at a hospital.

And, in 1990, I taught yoga for my first time ever, to the mentally- challenged. It was such a success that I was hired. And that's how I became a yoga teacher. Then I went on to teach the blind, the elderly, and those in wheelchairs.

There's not much to tell beyond that. To me, I had found true freedom. Before, I defined freedom as "fulfilling my desires," but I ended up a slave to desire. In my renewed life, I had nothing to hide because I stopped lying, I didn't have to watch my back because I had stopped stealing, I had no enemies because I no longer had bad intent toward anyone; rather, I wanted to *help* others. Sometimes I felt like I was walking on water. The world could not touch me. There were no entanglements, traps, nor double binds.

Now I really knew what freedom was: A state of mind.

~ ~ ~

You might say that my life, compared with the one years ago, became either wonderfully boring or marvelously normal. And yet my life has a deeper hue, an inner richness, just by my "being here now." I'm now content with the little things that fill my soul — fresh morning air, a walk on a country road, just feeling my breath as I meditate.

I've sometimes wondered, during this journey, *"Is my life meaningful?"* But I don't ask that anymore. In 1998, my son, Evan, was born. I'm someone's father. That makes me the most important person in the world to a little boy.

When I look at my son, I see God.

The world hasn't changed, but I have. Back in the days when I was really messed up, I blamed everyone and everything for my troubles. But *I* was the problem. In order to change the world I lived in, *I* had to change. My problems were not solved until I became the person who could solve them.

And I think that's Babaji's point. You can know all the wisdom and all the practices, but unless you apply them, they're useless.

Because, in the very end, you don't find "the answer"...

You become it.

Remember, the door to the sanctuary is inside of you.

~Rumi

Conclusion

Danny Paradise

We live in the world of maya whereby we only see a small part of the multidimensional reality we live in. Through my explorations of yoga and consciousness, I've come to recognize yoga as an ongoing, constantly-expanding exploration of this multidimensional reality. Yoga allows us to turn our dreams into living masterpieces, to constantly expand our boundaries, to break all conditioned patterns, and to step outside the regular order of life.

Yoga is about being a conscious witness as well as participant in life, whereby one can communicate directly with the Great Spirit, the heart of the universe herself. Yoga is an unlimited, spiraling, personal, evolutionary study. It is a form of shamanism, one of the oldest healing arts, where each one of us becomes our own authority on our personal evolution — our journey back to the Great Spirit.

The shaman is a lover of the sacred. They take those who appear at their doorstep and encourage them to enter. Their practices are empowering and expand the way we think, enabling those who enter to lead their lives with awareness so that they may accept responsibility for all that happens on their self-evolutionary path.

Shamanism is the practice of ecstatic ways of "knowing" and yoga is one of the many shamanistic ways we can reach this knowing. The Shramanas were an ancient sect of yogis/shamans who probably carried their ascetic practices throughout much of Asia, and there is some evidence of them being engaged in the ascetic heat-building disciplines of yoga in the Indus Valley over 5000 years ago. There, spending much of their days in deep meditation, they recognized that the yogi makes a personal, powerful connection with the Divine.

In my encounters with the spiritual traditions of indigenous cultures around the globe, including those of the natives of North and South America, Hawaii, and southeastern Asia and Africa, I've recognized similarities. These similarities suggest that while the vast teachings and practices of yoga that nurture communication with the Great Spirit may have been refined in India, they may have shamanic origins in China, in ancient Egypt, or even in the native cultures of the Americas. These teachings may have arisen independently of one another, or perhaps travelers journeying the globe shared this traditional wisdom with all they met.

In the Brazilian Amazon, the connection of yoga with shamanism was especially made clear to me, as shamanism comes from the principle that nature is our true teacher and spiritual guide. There, in the Amazon, and in indigenous Native traditions worldwide, the exploration of all levels of non-ordinary reality is considered a primary step in self-evolution. Considering themselves as protectors and restorers of nature, indigenous peoples see healing and communication with the spirit realms as of prime importance, along with their desire to live happily while helping mankind.

As in the deeper teachings of yoga, shamanism opens our perception to the multiple levels of reality, the eternal nature of life, and the illusion of what most Westerners feel is the finality of death.

Mayan Elders have stated that "kundalini," understood in the Mayan tradition for 100,000 years, is an empowering force within that aids our self-awareness. They called it Kuthalini, whereas in Central America it is described as Quetzlcoatl, the Great Spirit Messenger who rests as a coiled serpent at the base of the spine. When enlightenment or awakening occurs, the serpent power is said to rise up the spine as electrical energy in an explosive connection with the cosmos, creating transcendence and lifting us to a dimension beyond the mortal mind. Apparently as in death, where human consciousness fuses with the "Absolute" or "Divine Consciousness."

And in Egypt, ancient hieroglyphics with yogic poses have been found, demonstrating a clear understanding of the endless transmigration of the soul, the power of breath, of meditation, and of the nature of eternity. The root of their teachings describes the "intelligence of the heart" as being the only true guide and leader on this perilous path.

Rather than being about authorities or experts, gurus or priests, yoga is about accessing the deep-knowing within. Yoga is a foundation for living and is key in meeting the challenges of life, in creating our personal destiny, in aging with grace, health, and wisdom, and in approaching death with clarity and tranquility.

It is an ongoing, constantly-expanding exploration, the science of peace, meditation, healing, freedom, flexibility, strength, balance, breath and happiness; in essence, it is the science of being a "spiritual warrior." Such warriors, according to the Native Americans, are those who use their life energy to create a world of balance and harmony for our children, warriors who put energy into actions that help to both heal the Earth and to restore her balance.

The yogi is the "middle" man or woman between ordinary and non-ordinary reality, and the awakening that can occur during yoga represents the explosive force of kundalini on one's consciousness. Subtle expressions of awareness such as increased perception, increased intuition and increased insight are just the beginning; feeling freer and wilder comes next!

Yoga heals our mind, body and spirit, compelling us to act compassionately and tenderly in a world that needs this now more than ever. By coming completely into the present moment and eliminating stress and anxiety, we have endless opportunities and an open road ahead. As we restore and heal our own foundation, we can then access our true selves and create a healthier reality for both ourselves and the world.

Conclusion

Said the Buddha: *To straighten the crooked, you must first do a harder thing: Straighten yourself. You are your only master.*

We are each the stewards of our body, our mind, and our spirit, as well as our world; our bodies and minds are temporary gifts on loan to us from the universe. A humbling reality, indeed.

We are the inheritors of the universe, we are the ancestors of the future, we are both the Bodhisattvas and the Witnesses at the same time. Our work is to heal the wounded heart of both ourselves and the world.

The yogi sits in an erect position in Mahamudra, directly in communication with his or her own heart, mind and soul.

And with the Great Soul.

Contributors

Neal Arbic
~

Neal is a hatha yoga and meditation teacher, and author of... *Yoga for the Soul*. He began practicing and studying yoga over 27 years ago, trained and certified at California's Ashtanga Yoga Institute, and has been a full-time yoga and meditation instructor since 1990. Neal has appeared on TV and radio nationwide, has been offered positions with corporations such as Husky, Orenda Aerospace and Ford, and happily teaches in Caledon, Ont. when he is not online at www.becomingpeace.net.

Janet Aschkenasy
~

Janet is a financial writer and yoga teacher who directs the volunteer yoga teaching program at the Callen Lorde Community Health Center in Manhattan and teaches at Reflections Yoga near Times Square. She lives with her husband, Jimmy Napoli.

Katherine Culp
~

Katherine is working toward reaching enlightenment within this lifetime and says she may have to live much longer than the normal life span to do so! She has been painting and creating pretty much since the day she was born and works in the investment banking industry, painting water colors on the side. She hopes to retire soon and paint full-time while living in the beauty of nature.

Contributors

Reema Datta
~

Reema runs the Usha Yoga Foundation and teaches yoga worldwide. In an effort to remember these early teachings of using yoga to create world harmony, yogis around the world work with the Usha Yoga Foundation to bring yoga to remote areas as well as to battered women's shelters, old age homes, hospitals, and rehabilitation clinics. The idea for the foundation was sparked by Reema's grandfather, who has been practicing yoga for most of his 86 years and who now runs a yoga and community center in Khaknar, a tribal village in Central India. The foundation supports projects in India and worldwide. To learn more visit www.ushayogafoundation.org

Lorraine Gane
~

Lorraine Gane is a poet, writer, teacher, and editor on Canada's Salt Spring Island. Her poems, articles, essays, and reviews have been widely published across North America. She is the author of *Even the Slightest Touch Thunders on My Skin*, and is now working on a new volume, *The Blue Halo*. She teaches writing through online courses, private workshops, and at various universities. www.lorrainegane.com

Sharon Gannon
~

Sharon is the co-creator, with David Life, of the Jivamukti yoga method and is a pioneer in teaching yoga as spiritual activism — relating ancient teachings of yoga to the modern world. She is the author of several books and has produced numerous yoga-related DVDs and music CDs. She feels blessed by her teachers Sri Brahmananda Sarasvati, Swami Nirmalanda and Sri K. Pattabhi Jois. Learn more at www.jivamuktiyoga.com

Rabbi Joseph Gelberman
~

Rabbi Gelberman, a pioneer of the interfaith movement, founded New York's New Light Temple with Sri Swami Satchidananda and the Rev. Jon Mundy in the early 1970s. Ten years later, he helped establish The New Seminary for Interfaith Studies, the first of its kind to train interfaith ministers who could serve people of all faiths, and at age 87, he opened the All-Faiths Seminary International, a source of advanced spiritual education for clergy and professionals. A modern Hassidic rabbi, who ordained rabbis through his Rabbinical Seminary until his 98th year, Dr. Gelberman was also a dedicated yoga practitioner who wrote several books including *Physician of the Soul (A modern Kabbalist's Approach to Health and Healing)*. He auspiciously chose to leave this earthly plane on Sept. 9, 2010, during Rosh Hashanah, a time of rebirth and new beginnings for people of the Jewish faith.

Sabine Gifford
~

Sabine Gifford lives with her husband and daughter in the mountains of North Carolina, USA. Besides holding a Master's Degree in Education, a degree in life coaching and a yoga teacher certificate, she has added stay-at-home mom to her list of proud achievements.

Contributors

Linda Handiak
~

Linda Handiak is a high school teacher in Quebec. She has recently channelled her summer volunteering experiences into a book, *101 Green Travel Tips*, published by Life Tips. Her stories can also be found on the Matador Travel website and in the *Chicken Soup for the Soul* series.

Rosanne Harrison
~

After owning and operating a yoga and website business in Chicago, Rosanne received a Masters degree in secondary education and was an educator for six years in Chicago's public schools where she integrated yoga into the schools curriculum with great success. Currently, Rosanne is designing and researching a small high school model for her doctoral degree in Urban Educational Leadership with a focus in Curriculum Design. A major aspect of the model is the linking of yoga throughout all disciplines. Rosanne plans to open this small school in south Florida where she now lives with her young son and baby girl — both of whom have saved Rosanne, she says, from her restless nature!

Mariel Hemingway
~

Mariel is a veteran of over twenty movies, including *Manhattan*, (in which she was nominated for an academy award) *Lipstick*, *Personal Best*, and *The Contender*. She made her television series debut in the critically acclaimed Steven Bochco series *Civil Wars*, and earned a Golden Globe nomination for her performance.

She has also produced and starred in many environmental documentaries. When her love of health and yoga became paramount in her life, she turned to writing books such as *Finding my Balance*; *Mariel Hemingway's Healthy Living From the Inside Out* and *Mariel's Kitchen: Simple Ingredients for a Delicious and Satisfying Life* (published in 2009). She also has a company called Mariel's Kitchen whose products include Blisscuits (gluten-free organic cookies). She shares her love of healthy, happy living on her website, www.marielhemingway.com and in workshops and speaking engagements across the country.

Robert Knoss
~

Robert is a former UK investment banker whose health crisis with cancer propelled him to pursue a career in the field of nutrition (www.functionalnutrition.eu) and to do yoga teacher training. Iyengar yoga is an important part of his life, as are his many ventures on African safaris to quench his passion for wildlife.

Wade Imre Morissette
~

The twin brother of Alanis, Wade is a sought-after British Columbia-based yoga instructor and talented musician whose appeared on television and radio nationwide. In 2004, he took his debut album, *Sargam Scales of Music,* on the Lululemon Yoga Pilgrimage worldwide. In 2006, Wade signed on with Nettwerk Records to release his second album, *Strong as Diamonds: Om Vajra Kaya Namaha,* where he combined his two passions — yoga and music — to create an original blend of indie rock/pop music with Sanskrit and English chants. Wade is also a reiki master, certified Phoenix Rising yoga therapist and Viniyoga Therapist who can be found online at www.wadeimremorissette.com and on earth, teaching in Vancouver and around the globe.

Zo Newell
~

Zo discovered yoga at age 14 under the guidance of R.S. Mishra (Sri Brahmananda Sarasvati) of Ananda Ashram, New York. She later earned her Master's of Theological Studies from Harvard Divinity School with a focus on Indian religions, and is currently writing her dissertation for a Ph.D. in Vanderbilt University's Graduate Dept. of Religion. Her book on asana and personal development, *Downward-facing Dogs and Warriors: Wisdom Tales for Modern Yogis*, was published by the Himalayan Institute Press in September, 2007 (available at www.zonewell.com) and won a Nautilus Silver Medal for Book of the Year. She lives in Nashville, Tennesee, with her husband, James, and their three dogs.

Adelheid Ohlig
~

Formerly a journalist and editor for major news agencies, Adelheid has spent the past two decades as a Luna Yoga teacher and as a translator living in Switzerland. She has studied yoga and other body therapies since 1966, and has taught worldwide since 1983. Her book, *Luna Yoga,* describes her powerful method of healing in detail and is available in North America through Ash Tree Publishing or in Europe through Adelheid's multilingual website, www.luna-yoga.com.

Danny Paradise
~

Danny Paradise is a traveling Ashtanga yoga teacher who has practiced Ashtanga Yoga since 1976. He studied with the first Western teachers of Ashtanga, David Williams and Nancy Gilgoff in Hawaii, then with the father of Ashtanga yoga, Sri Patabbhi Jois. Danny has introduced Ashtanga Yoga to sports champions, film directors, and celebrities such as Sting, Paul Simon, Eddie Vedder, Graham Nash, Madonna and John McEnroe, and has taught yoga in all corners of the world. He draws from the teachings of Krishnamurti, Buddha, ancient Egypt as well as many indigenous cultures, and his life goal is to help people develop a sacred, joyful, meditative, pain free, personal self-practice. He is most easily found at www.dannyparadise.com

Martha Patt
~

Martha teaches yoga specifically for MS clients, including classes in San Francisco. On June 30, 2000, Martha was awarded her first grant from the Betaseron Champions of Courage. A subsequent award in 2002 from them allowed her to take the idea of yoga for MS patients to Denver and Chicago. Find her and more info about her DVD, *Yoga 4 MS,* at www.facebook.com/marthapatt

Father Joe Pereira
~

In 2009, Father Joe Pereira won a Padma Shri Award, granted by the Government of India to Indian citizens who have made a distinguished contribution in various spheres of activity such as social welfare and public life. He previously won the Mother Teresa National Award in 2008. In 1981, he founded the Kripa Foundation (now with fifty-one centres across India and four collaborative centres abroad), which includes yoga with psycho-spiritual and psycho-social aspects as in the twelve step program. In 2009, for the remarkable foundation's 25th anniversary, Father Joe produced a DVD and guide book by Medio Media—WCCM (World Community for Christian Meditation) titled *Yoga for the Practice of Christian Meditation* which addresses HIV/AIDS, addictions and more. He has also created a program teaching yoga for priests-to-be. Visit him at www.kripafoundation.org

Manuela Rohr
~

Manuela has been practicing and teaching yoga for over twenty years and is a certified Hatha Yoga Teacher by the German and European Yoga Association. She moved to the United States in 1987 where she continued her studies and became a Phoenix Rising Yoga Therapist in 1996. Manuela's personal path has been guided by a deep interest in self-awareness and self-expression, and her wish to support others in realizing their full potential. She lives with her husband and fabulous daughter, Sarina, in California and hopes to one day write a book about Sarina.

Sonny Rollins
~

Sonny Rollins, 80, will go down in history as not only the single most enduring tenor saxophonist of the bebop and hard bop era, but also as the greatest contemporary jazz saxophonist of them

all. His fluid and harmonically innovative ideas, effortless manner, and easily identifiable and accessible sound have influenced generations of performers. His latest CD, *Road Shows,* Vol. 1, was released in 2008. Rollins continues to performm worldwide and is the recipient of countless awards, most recently the rarely-bestowed Austrian Cross of Honor for Science and Art.
His online home is www.sonnyrollins.com

Russell Simmons
~

USA Today recently named Russell Simmons one of the "Top 25 Most Influential People of the Past 25 Years," calling him a "hip-hop pioneer" for his ground breaking vision that has influenced music, fashion, finance, television and film, as well as the face of modern philanthropy. From creating his seminal Def Jam Recordings in 1984, to the 2007 publishing of his New York Times best-seller *Do You! 12 Laws to Access the Power in You to Achieve Happiness and Success*, Russell is recognized globally for his influence and entrepreneurial approach to both business and philanthropy.

As Chairman and CEO of Rush Communications, Russell also leads the non-profit division of his empire, Rush Community Affairs, and its ongoing commitment to empowering at-risk youth through education, the arts, and social engagement. He also serves as UN Goodwill Ambassador For The Permanent Memorial To Honor The Victims Of Slavery and The Trans-Atlantic Slave Trade. Learn more about his phenomenal work at www.rushcommunications.com

Contributors

Sting

~

Sting has evolved into one of the world's most distinctive and highly respected performers. As lead singer and bassist for *The Police*, Sting, along with Andy Summers and Stewart Copeland quickly became a success, scoring several number one hits and five Grammy awards. As a solo artist, Sting has earned an additional eleven Grammys, two Brits, a Golden Globe, an Emmy, three Oscar nominations, *Billboard Magazine*'s Century Award, and was MusiCares 2004 Person of the Year. In 2003, he published a memoir entitled *Broken Music*, which spent thirteen weeks on the New York Times Best Sellers list. He has appeared in fifteen films, executive produced the critically acclaimed, *A Guide To Recognizing Your Saints,* and in 1989 starred in a Broadway play, *Threepenny Opera.* Along with wife Trudie Styler, Sting founded The Rainforest Foundation in 1989 to protect both the world's rain forests and the indigenous peoples who live there. Husband and father of six, masterful guitarist and bassist, he stays centered as a devoted yoga practitioner. Visit him at www.sting.com

Taz Tagore

~

Taz is an author and social entrepreneur who studied human biology and chemistry at Queen's University and received an MBA from Harvard Business School. She is renowned for her work with homeless persons via The Reciprocity Foundation (www.reciprocityfoundation.org), which she created and directs. The foundation uses spirituality, creativity and community to help break the cycle of poverty in the US. Taz has been featured in the *New York Times*, the *Wall Street Journal* and the *New York Post,* as well as television and radio, and is a featured parenting expert on Deepak Chopra's website. When not multi-tasking, she can be found writing her blog, *Innercubicle.*

Nance Thacker
~

Nance is a yoga practitioner and Certified Hypnotist based in Burlington, Ontario. Her practice incorporates Shiatsu Therapy, Lomi (Hawaiian Temple Bodywork), Lomilomi, Hypnosis, Soulwork and Dreamwork. She became a yoga teacher in 1976 in B.C. and Ontario, and says she was blessed to find her spiritual teacher during a Straightwalk workshop with Swami Radha, whose piercing insight and loving compassion touched her soul. She writes about the paradox of synchronicity, her cats and the wonder of life in her lively blog, *Awakening Choice,* available at www.awakeningchoice-nance.blogspot.com

Tracey Ulshafer
~

Tracey is the owner of One Yoga & Wellness Center in East Windsor and Ewing, New Jersey, (www.oneyogacenter.net) which holds yoga classes and teacher trainings. She gives free yoga classes to local charities in need, and looks forward to having more opportunities to work for her community in the future. Tracey aims to combine her passions for both yoga and writing as she continues her amazing journey. Her second self-published novel, *Wolf,* was released this year.

Amy Weintraub
~

Author of *Yoga for Depression* (Broadway Books) and founding director of the LifeForce Yoga Healing Institute, Amy leads professional certification trainings in *LifeForce Yoga for Depression and Anxiety* for mental health professionals and yoga teachers. She is also a senior Kripalu teacher (E-RYT 500) and Mentor, featured on the CD, *Breathe to Beat the Blues* and the DVD *Life Force Yoga to Beat the Blues*. She leads workshops and Continuing Education Units (CEU trainings) throughout North America at such venues as the Psychotherapy Networker Symposium, the American Holistic Medical Association's Annual Conference, and the Omega Institute. Her newsletter includes current research, news and media reviews on yoga and mental health. Let her cheer you up at www.yogafordepression.com

Permissions

"In Gandhi's Footsteps" by Sharon Gannon. From the prologue to her book *Yoga & Vegetarianism*. Mandala Press, 2008. Reprinted and adapted (edited) with permission of the author and publisher.

"My Yogic Blessing" by Mariel Hemingway, from her book *Finding My Balance*. Mariel Hemingway, Simon & Schuster, New York 2003. Reprinted and adapted with permission of the author and publisher.

"Coming Home" by Jane Hooper. Reprinted and shortened with permission of Kolin Lymworth, Banyen Books and Sound, Vancouver, BC.

"A Joyous Refuge" by Zo Newell, from her book *Downward Facing Dogs and Warriors*. Himalayan Press, 2007. Reprinted and adapted with permission of the author.

"Dancing with the Feminine" by Adelheid Ohlig. from her book, *Luna Yoga*. Ash Tree Publishing, 1994. Reprinted and adapted with permission of the author and publisher.

"Hip Hopping to Yoga" by Russell Simmons. Reprinted from *Do You! 12 Laws to Access the Power in You to Achieve Happiness and Success*. Russell Simmons with Chris Morrow. Gotham Books, 2007. Reprinted and adapted with permission of the author and publisher.

"The Holographic Life" by Sting. Reprinted from his foreword in *Jivamukti Yoga* by Sharon Gannon and David Life. Ballentyne Books, 2002. Reprinted and adapted with permission of the author and publisher.

"A House for My Soul" by Nance Thacker. Printed and adapted with permission from the author. A shorter version of this story was published in *Yoga Magazine*, July, 2007.

"Into the Light" by Amy Weintraub: The original version of this story was originally published in *Yoga for Depression: A Compassionate Guide to Relieve Suffering Through Yoga*, Amy Weintraub, Broadway Books, 2004. Reprinted and adapted with permission of the author and publisher.

Glossary

Ananda: "Bliss" in Pali, Sanskrit and other Indian languages. Often found as the ending of a swami's name, such as Yogananda.

Ashtanga yoga: A system of yoga popularized by Sri K. Pattabhi Jois.

Ayurveda: An ancient Indian system of medicine, it has been practiced for over 5,000 years and is said to heal patients based on their dosha (mind/body/spirit type). Includes the use of herbs, oils, massage, and yoga.

Bhagavad Gita: Also known as the "Song of God," it is part of the Mahabharata, written between 500 B.C.E. and 300 B.C.E., and is considered to be a sacred Hindu scripture and key text on yoga.

Guru: Spiritual guide or teacher. Regarded as a "remover of darkness."

Hassidic: A branch of Orthodox Judaism that maintains that God's presence is in all of one's surroundings, and emphasizes mysticism, prayer and joy.

Hatha Yoga: Includes all styles of the physical aspect of yoga such as Iyengar, Ashtanga and Power Yoga.

Hatha Yoga Pradapika: Light on the Union of the Sun and Moon, a practical treatise on Hatha Yoga describing asanas, kriya, mudras, bandhas and samadhi. A classic Sanskrit manual.

Integral Yoga: Founded by Swami Satchidananda. Combines raja yoga, japa yoga, hatha yoga, karma yoga, bhakti yoga, jnana yoga and the repetition of a mantra to reflect a comprehensive system of yoga.

Iyengar: A type of yoga popularized by BKS Iyengar, born Dec. 14, 1918, and introduced to yoga when a boy, by his guru: Sri T. Krishnamacharya.

Kabbalah: A set of mystical/esoteric teachings within Hassidic Judaism, meant to explain the nature of the universe and human beings, the nature and purpose of existence, and various other existential questions.

Krishnamacharya: T. Krishnamacharya Yoganjalisaram (1888-1989), regarded as the "father of modern yoga," he was the guru of BKS Iyengar, Sri K Pattabhi Jois, and TKV Desikachar. His fundamental principle was that yoga must always be adapted to an individual's changing needs for the individual to derive the maximum therapeutic benefits.

Krishnamurti: Born Jiddu Krishnamurti on May 11, 1895 in southern India. Krishnamurti did not expound any philosophy or religion, but travelled the world teaching about the need for a radical change in mankind, the subtle workings of the human mind, and the need for bringing a deeply meditative and spiritual quality to one's daily life.

Mudra: Symbolic gestures done predominantly with the hands in yoga.

Nadis: According to the tantras, there are 72,000 subtle channels or nadis carrying prana and the flow of consciousness throughout the body, the Ida, Pingala and Sushumna channels said to be of prime importance.

Om: Also written as *aum*, this sacred mantra is considered in Hinduism to be the vibration of the Supreme.

Paramahansa Yogananda: Author of the renowned *Autobiography of a Yogi* which outlines Yogananda's spiritual life from boyhood in India to his life in the US where he founded The Self-Realization Fellowship in 1920.

Patanjali: The "father of yoga," he authored the *Yoga Sutras*, considered to be the most authoritative of yoga texts. This work presents all of the concepts of yoga in 195 aphorisms, as well as the "eight limbs" of yoga.

Rishis: Described as Hindu sages, saints or Vedic seers who composed Rigvedic hymns, millenia ago.

Sadhana: Personal spiritual practice in which a person does yoga, meditation, prayer, chanting, etc.

Samadhi: The ultimate state of being/bliss which occurs when the meditator merges with the object of meditation; the eighth limb that Patanjali speaks of. in the *Yoga Sutras.*

Sanskrit: The ancient, sacred language of India and of yoga.

Satsang: A gathering of spiritual aspirants centered around a spiritual guide or teacher.

Sushumna: Also pronounced as sukhamana, it represents the central nadi or governing channel of energy in the body.

Siddha: A "liberated" being; the state desired by yogis.

Swami Vishnu Devanda: The Sivananda ashram was founded in 1967 by this swami, a legendary Hindu monk and yogi who arrived in North America in 1957 and, three years later, published *The Complete Illustrated Book of Yoga.* Sent by Swami Sivananda, Vishnu spread the discipline of yoga to North America.

Svadharma: One's personal path, which is based on one's own particular physical, mental and emotional nature, and the sum of past karmas.

T.K.V. Desikachar: A son and student of Krishnamacharya, Desikachar holds a degree in structural engineering, He is a world-renowned teacher of yoga, and founded the Krishnamacharya Yoga Mandiram (in Chennai, India) where he teaches with his son Kaustub.

Vedas: A huge body of texts originating in ancient India. The oldest layer of Sanskrit literature, and the oldest scriptures of Hinduism. Revealed to the first yogis through meditation, millenia ago.

About the Editor

Lisa quips that she began yoga at five years of age when her father placed her in headstands and put ceramic dishes on her soles to see how long she could balance them. She later turned to yoga to balance her life!

An avid yogini who aspires to be as healthy in her '90s as was Vanda Scaravelli, Lisa does yoga and reiki daily to remain grounded and to better the world through her writing and activism. Her articles on social, spiritual and health issues have appeared in *The Los Angeles Times, MacLean's Magazine, The Globe and Mail, The Toronto Star, Yoga Journal* and more, and as radio documentaries she produces based on many of these stories for Canada's *CBC Radio.*

Lisa is the passionate founder of an award-winning charity for youths, Artists Against Racism, and The Maya Hoffman Scholarship (*artspring.ca*) for child musical prodigies needing financial aid in Canada's Gulf islands. She also recently became a Street Yoga Teacher (*streetyoga.org*) to help inner-city youths and women in need, and is currently studying Storytime Yoga (*storytimeyoga.com*) to teach pre-teens so that they may have a balanced start in life. You may learn more about Lisa at: *lisacherry.ca, breathofyoga.blogspot.com,* and *artistsagainstracism.org.*

Photo: Brahm Fisher

249

Submit Your Story!

Meditate, chant, enjoy doing asanas daily while closing your eyes, gazing inward, and breathing deep ujjayi breaths. Then, write about *your* beautiful, wondrous journey, and email it to us for our next book or calendar!

Your Story

Stories from the Yogic Heart

Your Story

Stories from the Yogic Heart

Your Story

Email your *wondrous* story to yogicheart@gmail.com
or snail mail it to...

Yogic Heart Publishing
Box 54511
Toronto, Ont. Canada
M5M 4N5